Harriet Monroe

Valeria and other poems

Harriet Monroe

Valeria and other poems

ISBN/EAN: 9783742891495

Manufactured in Europe, USA, Canada, Australia, Japa

Cover: Foto ©Thomas Meinert / pixelio.de

Manufactured and distributed by brebook publishing software
(www.brebook.com)

Harriet Monroe

Valeria and other poems

Harriet Monroe

Valeria and other poems

VALERIA

AND OTHER POEMS

BY

HARRIET MONROE

CHICAGO

A. C. McCLURG & COMPANY

1892

THE CONTENTS.

VALERIA, A TRAGEDY.

POEMS. I.

II.

III.

IV.

SONNETS.

ENVOI.

ix

VALERIA

A TRAGEDY

IN A

PROLOGUE

AND

FIVE ACTS

Persons of the Prologue.

PRINCE ANDREA.

FLORIMOND, Count of Vancua, friend to the Prince.

GUARDSMEN.

VALERIA, a traveling child-minstrel and raconteur.

The action of the Prologue and of the Play takes place in one of the petty states of Italy during the fourteenth century.

PROLOGUE.

SCENE.—A roadside. In the distance a palace. Enter the child-
minstrel Valeria, ragged and weary, and bearing a lute.

Valeria.

How tired the day is, and my head is hot —
So hot perchance the sun has sent his beams ⌣
To rest upon it.   All the birds have flown.
Give me your wings, my music-makers — wings!
And I will seek you where the perfumes grow,
In the king's garden yonder.   I will see
The great white towers you wheel about, and hear
The voice of princes and of white-skinned maids.
Are you not happy when you die, my birds —
You who have seen such glory?   I believe
I could be joyous all my life if once
Some youth, all gold and velvet and perfume,
Like him who far away in yesterday ⌣
Reined in his steed to listen to my song —
If some such lord should take me by the hand

3

And say : I will not give thee coins for song —
Sing me a ballad for an hour of joy ;
One song, and for an hour thou shalt command,
And all the glories of thy dreams are thine !
Then would I shout and bid my laughing soul
Change to a princess for a lily's year ;
And I would cry, My robes, my jewels, ho !
Summon my slaves and bid them bear me on
Through gardens richer than a rose's heart,
Through halls where bright deeds, deeply set in gold,
Shine from the walls like jewels, and great kings
Stand forth in marble and at last are still.
Oh, I would crowd such years into that hour
That all my life would be but memory
And all my songs an echo !

[*She sings.*]

Have you heard of the princess who far away
   In a tower by the moaning sea
For her lover kept watch, till she heard one say
   That a perjured soul had he ?
For the troth she had plighted for aye, for aye,
   Was a jest to his spirit free.

One flash from her eyes, and she turned their light
   On the storm-bound sea and sky —
One moment, and swift through the pitiless night
   A shadowy shape sped by.
And no sound was heard, through the storm's affright,
   Of a human soul's last cry.

4

It is strange
The high-born princess could not find delight,
Whom all obeyed save one. Ah! would to Heaven
That I might wear her robes and coronet,
And have a troop of courtiers at my beck!
I would be happy as the bird that flies
Nearest the sun, content to fly alone.
No man of all their tribe should e'er disturb
My high serenity.

[The girl wanders out. Enter the Prince and Florimond, gay
youths laughing together.]

The Prince.
But, Florimond,
While there are horses in my father's realm
I cannot think of women.

Florimond.
Say you so!
Your highness then shall give me all the maids
And I will get you steeds from Barbary.

The Prince.
These ladies of the court, my Florimond,
Think you a man may find one maid of all
Whose whole life owns as much of nature's law
As yonder thrush's song? Oh, I am tired
Of the bowed heads and bending knees of women

5

Who spy the prince afar, but have no eyes
Save for his trappings! If I could but find
One face unconscious as the new-born day,
With eyes that to our noon in midnight bring
Swift visions of the morn, whose glances rise
Fearless as sunlight to encounter darkness,
A voice that blows like spring's fresh breezes through
Our hot-house bloom of courts, a step as free
As the wild mountain goat's, a heart untaught
And so untainted — find me such a maid
And she shall wear a crown! Yea, though her brow
Knows not the touch of gold, save when the sun
Beats amorous kisses on it.

Florimond.

But, my lord,
You do them wrong, the ladies of the court,
To hold them slaves to ceremony. Think
If you exact it not. You wear your rank
Even as the porcupine his spears, that wound
The unwary handler. Fold it by awhile,
This proud reserve and ill-advised scorn,
And search some lady's eyes for gentle proof
Of nature's rule in her. Trust me, your highness
Will fathom secret depths untroubled by
Windy frivolities of etiquette.
But when you find that peerless maid, my lord,
Untaught, untainted, free — you know the rest —

6

Methinks I would not crown her, lest perchance
Her wild charms stifle in our fevered air.
It is enough to give such lowly grace
The left hand of your favor, for the state
Claims the bestowal of your right, and asks
No queen so savage.

The Prince.

                    By this sword I swear
The state that owns me for its king will take
The queen I give it, though her voice be tuned
Unto a beggar's whine, and though her robes
Be ragged as the tatters of old Time.
And you may tell the councilors of state
No woman whom I love shall be deceived
With that base homage which the rotting time
Pays to king's mistresses.   I do not wish
To join the crowd of noble dissolutes
Who sicken states with rank airs of dishonor,
Till strength and glory fall to leprosy
And ruin undermines the very throne.
My country has my service ; to her cause
I dedicate my hands, my brain, my life.
I serve her so devoutly it were treason
To give my heart to any save her queen.

Florimond.

'T is well for kings all patriots think not so.

The Prince.

Your honor's gone a-jesting.

Florimond.

Nay, I applaud
Your ardor in preparing bandages
To bind the wounds of Time, and make him whole.
His is a scarred old visage; nevermore
The eyes of youth will open on the world,
All innocence and wonder. Since our age
A sour and wrinkled tyrant is, 't were wise
To wear his colors, and not flaunt abroad
The flaring virtue of your youth.

The Prince.

My friend,
Ah! be not thus the spokesman of the time,
And voice the message that the very air
Is heavy with. Truth has been drugged so long
She hangs her head in shame, and men forget
The glory in her eyes. But some there are
Who search them still, and the white-souled old priest
Who taught me long ago was one of these.
He tore away the veil of sophistries
And gave me one deep look into her soul,
And I can not forget. Ah! Florimond,
She yet will conquer! In a fight with her
Our age would infamously perish. Come:

Shall we not greet her in all friendship, ere
She falls upon her foes?

Florimond.
                    A miracle!
A prince in love with truth!   A despot's son
Hoping to rule by righteousness!   My lord,
May hosts of angels aid you, for I fear
Earth's soldiers will not!

The Prince.
                    'T is a merry tune —
This song of yours!

Florimond.
                    But I will give you time.
A few years near the throne will wear away
The antique wisdom of the priest —

The Prince.
                              No more!
A pestilence is sweeter than your tongue!
I have no taste for rankness, so will leave you
To your amusing thoughts.

Florimond.
                    I have presumed.
Friends must be frank, my lord.

The Prince.

If you are frank,
Heaven mend your soul and guard your loyalty !

[Exit the Prince.]

Florimond.

So fierce — so fierce !   I 'd rather be a child
Than own a spirit rigid as a post,
And pointing one way always.   Faugh ! he lies
Secure within my hand.   Good saints in heaven !
'T is the same Psyche in the beggar's robe.
Now for an ambush.   So.

[Valeria reappears.]

Valeria.

Alas ! alas !
Why must I dream of kings and palaces,
And wear these rags, sleep 'neath the staring stars,
And learn new songs forever till I die !
Oh, I must think no more.   A song ! a song !
Best dance and sing, and so wear out the day.

[*She sings and dances wildly.*]

Dance on, children of song, over the hills with me ;
Haste down, out of the clouds, down to the sunlit sea.
Wild winds sweep us afar out of the heights they sway.
Ah, come ! breathe of the south, buried in blue — away !

Come, win kingdoms of light ; crown ye with summer's
praise.
Sing ! dance ! tune me your lutes, wreathe them with deathless bays. +

Are ye beggars that rove, heirs of the proud world's scorn ? +
Nay, kings! dowered with wealth richer than gold of morn.

[Reënter the Prince, who listens unnoticed.]

On, on ! Ours is the truth ; deep in her heart we read.
We give glory to fame, life to the mighty deed.
Gods we — conquering death, wreathing his brow with
  flowers.
Give earth all to her slaves—heaven and time are ours!

Then dance — far and away —

[She reels, overpowered by the heat.]

Where is the song gone? Oh, my heart! my heart!
God! is this death ?

[She falls fainting. The Prince hastens to her and raises her head on
  his knee. Florimond approaches.]

The Prince.

Some water, Florimond !

Florimond.

Here 's wine, my lord.

[The Prince forces wine into her mouth, but she does not revive.
  He then blows a signal on his bugle twice, which is repeated from
  the palace far away.]

The Prince.

She is more beautiful
Than is the face of glory to the brave.   +

Florimond.

More fair than death. ✗

The Prince.

Be still—she is not dead!
No Spartan girl could sing her soul to sleep
With words so like life's song of triumph.　Look!
See you the horsemen?

Florimond.

Down the road I see
Their plumes lie prone upon the wind for speed. ✗

The Prince.

Her voice was like the dawn across a sea,
Making the old world quiver with new light. ✝
God! thou wilt not eclipse it!

Florimond.

The sun was jealous,
Viewing in her a rival luminary
Which he must conquer ere the world be shaken
✗　From its proud balance.　Will you dare undo
His scorching work, unveil those dangerous eyes,
So harmless now?

The Prince.

Have we another Helen
In this poor child, and would you let her die

That the brown world may hold its smooth career?
Nay, nay—not all of us together reach
The value of such beauty.   Ah! they come!

[Enter, on a gallop, six or eight guardsmen with an officer, who
swiftly dismounts and salutes.]

Back, half of you, and from the palace hither
Bring food, wine, water, leeches, and a litter.
Haste, as you love me!   You who stay, approach,
And make your arms a couch.   We 'll follow them
Far as the spring and dew these secret eyes. ✦
Lightly as a young lily rises up
From the dull blackness of ancestral earth
Does she escape her fate in these our arms.

Florimond.

To be the fire-brand in fate's hand, perchance.

The Prince.

Ay, or the torch, to scatter healing light
Among the foul illusions of our time.

[Exeunt omnes.]

[*Curtain.*]

Persons of the Play.

THE KING.

PRINCE ANDREA, son to the King.

FLORIMOND, Count of Vancua, friend to the Prince.

COUNT LEONE, friend to the Prince.

AGNOLO, a courtier.

FILIPPO, a courtier.

CARDINAL ORTUS.

CAPTAIN of the King's Guard.

COURTIERS, GUARDSMEN, SOLDIERS, CITIZENS.

LIPERATA, sister to the King.

TORA, her daughter.

PIERA, friend to Tora.

OLIVIA.

VALERIA, musician and raconteur in the King's court.

LADIES OF THE COURT, WOMEN OF THE PEOPLE, AND DANCING GIRLS.

Five years elapse between the Prologue and the opening of the Play.

ACT I

ACT I

SCENE.—The garden of a palace at night. Lights hang in the trees, and beautiful statues, fountains, and flowers are visible. Enter the old and gray Cardinal Ortus with Florimond, who carries negligently a mask and domino.

Florimond.

And so you think the honor of our house
Sleeps in my charge.

Cardinal.

Say rather dies, my lord.
I have been silent till each drop of blood
Your father lost seems like a ghost in arms,
And all rise to reproach me. I have watched
While you bedraped that princeling like his cloak,
Breathing his sighs, urging your willing wit
To whet his laughter, and have said no word
Because I thought no scion of your race
Could live long in dishonor. But it seems
Red blood is water in your veins. You owe
No fealty to the dead. You have forgot
This king is but a tyrant, who betrayed

19

Freedom, and killed your father like a dog.
What other state in Italy would thus
Endure him ?   Who, the head of a great house,
Would let his father's blood rot unavenged,
And revel with his foes ?

Florimond.

Where is the proof
Of such grave charges ?

Cardinal.

Proof ! That mask and gown
Are proof enough.   You are a courtier here.
You let them drag you from his very bier
To fix you in the palace, load your back
With precious favors — take you to their hearts,
And so efface the stain, the memory
Of that great wrong.   By heaven ! 't were nobler far
To seek an exile in the desert plains
Of Africa, than here to live enriched
And be their friend.

Florimond.

You are too hot, my lord.
What if I too remember, seem their friend
But for an end?

Cardinal.

I tried to hope so once ;
But years have stretched my hope out to a hair,
And now even that has snapped.

Florimond.
What is the cause?

Cardinal.
Love is the cause. You love Valeria —
A beggar whom this prince plucked from the highway
To be his plaything.

Florimond.
And if I do, again
What is the cause?

Cardinal.
She is adroit, ambitious.
You are oblivious, and to gain your end
Would give o'er all, and marry her, and live
In slothful servitude forever.

Florimond.
Ho!
You need not fear. The house of Vancua
Will never stoop so low. Ah, you are blind!
Think you, if love were all of life to me
The rattling tongues of gossips would be weary
With jesting on my passion? Be assured
I can be secret when I choose. The fools —
They must have food for chatter — should I starve
Their eager appetites they might assail
The stronghold of our secrets. 'T is for this

I stuff them with a show of burning love
For the king's minstrel ; feeling, I confess,
Tender enough to make the semblance sweet.
No more of that ! By heaven ! your bitter words
Would anger me, were I not overjoyed
To find you still so ardent.

Cardinal.
                              You have had
No cause to doubt my ardor.   In this court
I hold no office, take no gold of theirs,
Give them no bows, no laughter.

Florimond.
                              By my sword, ✝
Think you I am a baby to be whipped?
What if I tell you that the lagging years,
By you passed in lamenting, have by me
Been consecrated to our sacred cause !
No word that I have uttered — ay, no jest
That I have shot into the frivolous ears
Of the young prince, but has availed me much
In power.   Where would our vengeance sleep to-day
If I had worn my hatred as a cloak
To keep me warm in exile ?   Like a cedar
Firm-rooted and strong-hearted would arise
The green strength of their rule, secure against
The black looks of unweaponed enemies.

22

I tell you, sir, this growth which seems so fair,
This kingdom that now shakes its leaves aloft
In the clear air of nations, in whose shade
The earth smiles with new fruitfulness,—I say
'T is hollow with disease. One blow from me
And it will fall.

Cardinal.
                    Is not the moment ripe
For such a blow ? Why will you idly see
Their throne cemented by these victories ?
To-morrow brings the prince in triumph home,
Lauded and garlanded. Your brow is bare,
Though well the soldier's laurel would become
Such liberal youth.

Florimond.
                    Where are your thoughts, my lord ?
I will not fight their battles, and besides,
This king, who thinks he has lulled my soul asleep,
Were but a fool to send it to the wars
And bid it waken in the clash of arms.
Ah, no! he loves me with such constancy
I must be always near him, though the fight
Should fail for lack of me. The old basilisk
Would charm me by his glance. He fears my wings
If once I try them. He does not suspect,
Nor you, how free I am, how strong I shall be.
I can be patient. While he wastes his power

In irritating wars, paying for glory
The people's loyalty, I stand aloof
And urge the impatient crowd to secret hate,
Waiting the hour when I may lead them on
To revolution.

Cardinal.

You are working, then?

Florimond.

I have not lost an hour since you and I
Received my father's heritage of wrong.
This very night I might escape the palace —
I have a friend among the sentinels —
And hasten to our friends, who often meet
To hear my secret words of hope and wrath.
Say — have you done so much?

Cardinal.

Alas, my son,
Forgive me if I saw no other course
Save exile for my honor. I 've no skill
To play a double part. I should betray
The hatred in my heart and lose us all.
You know not how reluctantly I wear
Even for a day the mask of friendship here.
They told me you were sunk in lethargy,
Dead to your honor. I had watched in vain
For any sign of life from you, and so

I came to tell you who you are.   But now
I know that you remember, and my soul
Which stifles here will seek its liberty.
To-morrow I depart.

Florimond.

Can you not gain
His Holiness to aid our cause?

Cardinal.

The pope?
I bear congratulations to the king
From him.   His thoughts are centered nearer home —
He would not listen.

Florimond.

If you only knew
How cruel is this secrecy, how blindly
Dense clouds of doubt envelop me, which seem
To cover an abyss where I must fall!
I hold the reins o'er many foaming steeds
That dash along a precipice.   My hands
Grow weary of the strain ; yet if they tremble
Our hope is ruin.   Lend me your arms awhile,
And we will hatch a plan shall make them dance —
These sanguine fools!

Cardinal.

What would you have me do?

25

Florimond.

I would present you to our friends, and say:
Three thousand men-at-arms in his domain
Ignobly toil, who wait our call alone
To march to our deliverance. Bid them come!
Be brave for freedom, rouse your laggard wrath,
Strike the usurper! Sir, I never dreamed
Of liberty if that were not enough
To arm her for the battle.

Cardinal.

All I have
Is yours for this good cause — five thousand men
Instead of three. My treasure all is yours,
My voice as well, though little skill is mine
To move the vulgar to my purposes.
Do with me as you will.

[Laughing voices are heard approaching. Cardinal Ortus and
   Florimond retire a little, Florimond covering himself with his
   domino. Enter, gaily talking, a troop of masked revelers —
   Piera, Tora, Valeria, Filippo, and others.]

Piera.

He slipped us here.

Florimond.

They must not find my father's friend and me
So close in talk. The king has jealous eyes
Under his brow of clemency.

Valeria.

Forbear!

He is the son of darkness — he is gone
To join his father Night.   We 'll search no more!

Filippo.

His father Night is here, yet he is not.

Piera.

Night has devoured his offspring then ; I know
He fled to it. ⊁

Valeria.

O parent pitiless!

Was that thy greeting ?

Filippo.

Out of the peril, then.

[Filippo tries to hold back Valeria; but she escapes him, runs
  across stage, and out at the other side, followed with wild
  laughter by the rest.]

Cardinal.

You know that voice!

Florimond.

It is Valeria.

Cardinal.

You are in danger, Florimond.   Beware
Lest honor's drum and cymbals stir your blood
Less than the reed of love.

Florimond.

You are suspicious.
This flower upon my breast will not retard
My march to yonder white-browed mountain-top.

Cardinal.

No, but to lie upon a bank of flowers,
Breathing their soporific soft perfumes,
Will much retard your march.   And I do fear
This beggar of the court.   Her eyes burn low,
Smoldering a fire that one provoking touch
Will quicken into soul-consuming flame.
Ah, son, love is the death of great designs — ✝
Destroy it !

Florimond.

Cardinal, it is repose.
If I lie lazy in the lap of love
'T is but the lion dreaming.

Cardinal.

Long ago
A hero dreamed thus idly, and awoke
Shorn of his strength.

Florimond.

He was a fool as well.
Content you, Cardinal.   And now make haste
Back to the palace, for I hear them coming.
Soon I will follow.

28

Cardinal.

If I trust you not

There is no hope.   Think of your father's blood —

Be true.

Florimond.

My father's blood be on my head

If I have lied !

Cardinal.

There speaks the Vancua !

Man, I will doubt no more — my hand upon it.

Florimond.

Good-night.

[Exit the Cardinal.]

How fierce he is to eat unripe

The fruit I shall watch mellow on the bough

Before I touch it — time enough and more

For soft encounters with Valeria.

Surely she is the daintiest thing that ever

Tempted the lips of princes.   All is still —

They have forsook the search, gone to the palace.

Now will the hare turn hunter.

[Enter Valeria stealthily.   A lute is slung over her shoulder.   She
is startled at seeing him.]

Valeria.

Ah, my lord,

You are a favorite ; a moment since

A dozen revelers scoured the darkness for you.

You 'll find them at the palace.

Florimond.

Sweet tormentor,
What do I care for revels, save when you
Make light and music of them ?   Do not think
Now to escape me.   Do you know how long
The weary days have chased the nights away
Since you and I have found an hour alone ?

Valeria.

Alas, my lord, twice hath the sky grown black
To mourn the muteness of your passion.

Florimond.

Nay —

It seems a weary year, for every hour
Thine eyes do not illumine wears for me
Night's black complexion.   O Valeria,
Thy beauty is the sun of my delight.
Why does it always wear a veil of frowns
Or smiles more cold ?

Valeria.

My lord knows it is death
To stand in the hot sunlight of the south.
I would not kill him with unguarded favor —
Therefore his skies are gray.

Florimond.

But I would toss
Life to the winds to feel but one swift flash
Of such unutterable rapture.

Valeria.

No,

Life is too dear a thing to toss away.
I fear me death has heard your bold defiance
And but awaits my yielding to accept it.

Florimond.

Oh, you are flippant as the summer winds!
I will not bow forever at the breath
Of your wild coquetry.   Mock me no more!
Hear me — I love you.

Valeria.

What my lord says now
He oft has said before.

Florimond.

But nevermore
Will he be paid with folly.   If my love
Rise to your heart in rapture, you are mine —
Now — ever!   If you spurn it you shall know
The force of what you spurn.   This is the end.
I am no dangler of the court, content
To take one smile in twenty, to be paid
For my heart's wealth with laughter.   Give me now
All that I ask, or by the saints —

Valeria.

My lord —
And if I loved a man of ancient name,
High in the state — the plume in fortune's cap,

What would it profit my unworthiness,
Whose ancestry was heedless as the birds,
That think of naught but song?

Florimond.

It might avail,
If he you loved could soar to heaven with you,
To set an earthly title on that brow
Imperial nature crowned with beauty.

Valeria.

Ah!
Too many voices call you, and to all
You lend a willing ear. To-night 't is love,
And the enchanting music of his lute
Lulls you to dreams till you forget the world.
To-morrow glory will awake your soul,
And love will be forgotten.

Florimond.

Say you so?
My ship is anchored in the harbor there.
Come — let us sail to-morrow far away,
And hear love's voice forever!

Valeria.

Know you not
I am the plaything of the court, the jester
These idle nobles bandy words with? Faugh!
A little petted by the king — permitted

Close to his ear, because my voice is sweet
And songs delight his soul. But have you noted
How the great ladies kindle to disdain
If my heart bounds across the chasm between us?
They suffer me for laughter or for song,—
'T is the king's will, forsooth, and must be borne,—
But never fellowship. Hast thou seen this,
And durst thou try to lift me to their rank,
When failure means thy shame?

Florimond.

Valeria,
Beyond the waters many a kingdom lies
Beside whose spacious acres this our country
Is but a handsbreadth. Let us sail away,
And seek great kings who know of thee and me
Naught save the name they cannot choose but honor.
There shall thy beauty shine unclouded; there
The rank God gave thee men shall not dispute—
These heathenish men, who see how fair thou art,
And ask some other proof of noble race
Than eyes divinely lit, hair all aglow,
A voice from heaven's own choir, and cheeks that flush
Even now to feel the breath of homage. Come!
And we will drift across long languid days,
And feel the salt wind on our brows, and watch
The red sun bear his train into the sea,
And leave the sky aglow with stars. Ah, come!
Hence on white wings to paradise!

33

Valeria.

I fear
Thy words have white wings, for my soul is borne
Half way to paradise already.

Florimond.

Ah!
Thou lov'st me then?

Valeria.

Thou canst not guess how long
Thy face has haunted me. A child was I
When thou didst check thy steed, and wait, and gaze,
And listen to my song. The coin thou threwest —
See, I have kept it, though I hungered oft
And this would buy a feast. I hungered oft,
But death seemed easier than the loss of it.

Florimond.

I too remember well that day, dear love.
My heart was surfeited with shows of things
When thy voice spake from heaven unto my soul,
And taught mine ears the sweeping harmonies
Thy spirit caught afar. Ah! sing me now
One song that I may treasure as mine own,
That none have heard nor shall hear. Let thy heart
Confess to me in melody. I wait
To hear how well thou lov'st me.

Valeria.

Ask no more!
How do I know if this be love which shines
Alluring as a torch? My fate has bowed
To such strange thoughts. Even when I saw thee first
Thy splendor dazed my soul, and evermore
The thought of thee suggested palaces
And kings and fair maids feasting in delight,
And filled my heart with longing and despair.
But was this love of thee or love of me,
Who can remember not one day of life
Unwarmed by hot desire of greatness? Ah!
Oft in my mother's arms beside the sea
My sobs have met the moaning of the waves
For all earth's glory that I might not share;
And when I wandered forth to sing, my voice
Was freighted with this passion, and would bear
Swift thought beyond the dust of humble ways,
To walk with kings. 'T is so even here — to-day.
Now that old dreams are firm realities
New fancies float above them, and perchance
If those were mine not yet would sweet content
Brush off the dust from eyes grown blind to truth.

Florimond.

Let love perform that office! He alone
Has power to wake thy life to happiness.
The longings of the old time and the new

35

Were but vague gropings toward his glorious light.
This bright dawn will absorb the vapors, sweet,
Thy rich imaginings—ah, let it rule!
Look in my eyes and say thou hast forgot
Time and the luring world.

Valeria.   [With steadfast gaze.]
                                    Upon my soul
I think I love thee.

Florimond.
                    Nay, I know thou dost.
Now let the world grow gray—our hearts are gold!
This for immortal joy!

                    [He kisses her.]

Valeria.   [Shuddering.]
                        Immortal!   Ah!
To-day is ours; to-morrow—who shall tell
If God or devil grasp it?   It is strange—
There is some boding in my deepest heart.
But—dost thou truly love me?

Florimond.
                            Love!   The rose
Less dear is to the bee than thou to me.

Valeria.
And wilt thou ever?

Florimond.
                    While my soul has breath.

36

Valeria.

Speak not so lightly.

If thou lov'st me then
Go back and seek the masquers.   Leave me here.
Go — I must be alone!

Florimond.

What dost thou mean?

Valeria.

I mean a thousand things — I mean — my head
Is whirling and must think.   Oh, do not tarry!
Wilt thou deny my little first request?

Florimond.

Nay, but what means this sudden swift alarm?
The hour is peaceful.   'Neath the tent of night
We may prepare our wings for flight.

Valeria.

Not now —
To-morrow, not to-day.

Florimond.

To-morrow eve
Our boat shall sail away —Oh, pledge me that!

Valeria.

Soon, soon, my lord, if you deny me not.
Good-night!

Florimond.

I 'll not deny thee.   Give me now
The jewel of thy love set in a song,
And I will leave thee, bearing in my heart
So rich a dower a king might envy me
That pearl of memory and hope.

Valeria.

A song ?
Thou hast it then !

[She sings softly, at first slowly and searchingly, then rapidly
and with intense enthusiasm.]

I love thee — my heart
    Hath its secret no more !
I love thee ; thou art
    All of earth I adore.
Thy strength is my shield
    And thy glory my crown.
To thy keeping I yield
    Thought, desire, and renown.

Three treasures I bring,
    Like the wise men of old
Who gave to our King
    Myrrh, incense, and gold.
Here is beauty for wealth,
    And for perfume a song :
Tears for myrrh fall by stealth
    From a rapture too strong.

38

Come, take me ! My soul
To thy search is laid bare,
And thy touch doth control
All my life unaware.
I love thee — and thou —
If thy vows are but truth,
What 's the world to us now?
What is time to our youth ?

Florimond. [Seizing her and gazing in her eyes.]
Turn to me ! look at me !
Am I a block that you should sing such words,
And gaze in air ?

Valeria.
Loose me—what did I say ?

Florimond.
Woman or sphinx, what art thou—stone or fire ?

Valeria.
Oh, leave me ! leave me ! Do not think of me !

Florimond.
My soul shall think of nothing else forever,
My changeling. 'T is thy blessing or thy curse,
Whichever thou shalt choose.

Valeria.
Wilt thou not go ?

Florimond.

Thou dost but dream, thou merciless, virgin thing.
To teach thee what love is—that would be brave
Beyond man's power. A god or fool might do it.
I look into thine eyes and hardly dare.
There 's something in thy soul love must beware,
A mortal challenge. I will answer it—
Adore thee, conquer thee, and make thee mine.

Valeria.

Or kill me.

Florimond.

Mine or death's. Ay, thou shalt choose
Me or the grave.

[Exit Florimond.]

Valeria.

Fool! fool! what have I done?
I do not love him thus—no, no—not thus!
Why did I sing? There is enchantment in it—
This music makes me mad! Alas! alas!
What wild words did I utter—and to him!
That man has cast a spell about me; yet
I dare not call it love, save when his eyes
Are gazing into mine, and all the world
Seems far away and buried in the past.
Let me forget it all, and close my lips
Lest witchcraft force a song from them.

                              The prince —
I had almost forgot the prince's order.
But 't is the hour and I am here alone —
Yet through what chances!   If the messenger
Had found him here!
                    I wonder what the prince
Desires of me, that he should send to-night
A special courier from the slumbering host —
The gentle prince, who seems so like a child,
And yet wins battles!   Let me read again
The note he sent me.

[Takes a paper from her pocket.]

                    At the hour of twelve
Be near the thicket in the grounds alone.
There one will meet thee from the prince, who hath
Much to inform thee of.   Alone — be faithful.

It is past twelve.

[The Prince has entered quietly at rear, in mask and domino.   Approaching, he removes his mask, and softly seizes the paper from her hand.]

                    The Prince.
                Behold the messenger!

                    Valeria.
Your highness!

                    The Prince.
            Hush!

41

Valeria.

What means this ?

The Prince.

I could trust
No other lips to-night.   How true thou art!
I knew thou wouldst be here.

Valeria.

Alas, my lord!
I am a thing inconstant to all else
Save this mad music that enslaves me so.

The Prince.

Nay, do not wrong thyself.

Valeria.

The truth can do
No wrong.   What wouldst thou say to me?

The Prince.

My heart
Is busy with old dreams, Valeria.

Valeria.

Your highness has the power—the power.   Ah me!
You need not dream.

The Prince.

But dost thou know my dream?

Valeria.

Old fires rekindle, old ambitions flash
To flame in this great triumph — is it this?

The Prince.

Would such thoughts bring me here disguised, alone,
Where glory will receive me open-armed
To-morrow?

Valeria.

Let my praises be the first.
You have been brave indeed, and all the world
Is trumpeting your fame.

The Prince.

Speak not of that.
Thy praise the jewel is in glory's crown,
But do not give it now.   My soul is filled
With humbleness to-night.   The waves of triumph
May bear me high to-morrow, but not now.
I have done nothing, or so poor a thing
It is not worth a breath, except—

Valeria.

Except?

The Prince.

One blessing it has brought, so dear, so sweet,
Power cannot rival it, though I should make
This hill the center of the world.

Valeria.

And that —

The Prince.

Hast thou not guessed? You women, I have heard,
Scent out these precious secrets of our hearts.

Valeria.

I am too little womanly, your highness —
Alas — too little womanly!

The Prince.

Thou art
The only woman in the world for me.
This is my message — I have come to say
I love thee.

Valeria.

Oh, be merciful!

The Prince.

But why
Am I unmerciful?

Valeria.

You love me — you?

The Prince.

What! am I more or less than man to thee?
Have I no eyes for beauty, and no heart
To waken to love's music?

Valeria.

Say no more —
I cannot bear it.   You have ranked so high
In my soul's gratitude — how can I live
And hear dishonor from you ?   Heaven knows
I have beheld the rampant vice of the time,
But never hugged it.   Have you found a charm
To make it lovelier ?   If your highness please,
No more of this !   Why did you send for me ?

The Prince.

Not for dishonor — by my soul I swear it !
I have no thought thou mayst not share.   My heart
Lies open to thy questioning.

Valeria.

And yet
You speak of love between us — between us ?

The Prince.

Thou know'st not how my heart has ached with it
For five long years, and yet has made no sign
Lest the hot breath of slander should assail thee.
I loved thee from the first.   I never knew
A thought of women till I heard thy song
And saw the sunlight of thy face go out
And leave all dark in the world.   But since that hour
One hope has been the purpose of my life,

The star that guided all my striving. Now
It leads me to the gates of paradise,
And thou shalt open them.

Valeria.
Upon my soul,
My lord is in a jesting mood to-night —
I understand him not.

The Prince.
Is it so strange
That I should throw my fortunes at thy feet ?
If thou but knew how I have worked for this,
How I have planned, fought, labored, though the sun
Shone hot upon my youth, and bade me pause.
My jewels of renown are all for thee ;
My victories are thine — they have been won
To make thy crown the brighter, for at last
I have the right to wed thee.

Valeria.
Are you mad ?
What mean you ? Me, a beggar — me, a weed
Plucked from the highway ! You would marry me ?
Impossible ! You have forgot the king.

The Prince.
I have forgotten nothing. Dear my heart,
Why dost thou doubt me ? Do I love deceit ?

46

Valeria.

No, no, I cannot doubt you, though my mind
Gropes blindly and in vain.

The Prince.
                    Then will I lead it
Forth to the light, for I will tell thee all.
My father loves me ; he who seems so cold
Keeps yet his heart green for his son, and fresh
With constant thoughts strewn o'er a grave long closed.
He loves me, and the subtle power of love
Can bend the will of kings, Valeria.
Thus did I gain thy entrance to the court,
The usage due a maid of rank for thee,
And all that nurture of thy highest thought
Which makes men marvel at thy learning now,
And seek thee more than princesses.   Through all
I guarded well the secret of my love.
'T was but a whim, forsooth, this wondrous child —
Too beautiful for soiling in the dust,
A voice too rich to beat the vacant air
When courtly ears are longing for a song ;
And such a mind — 't were profitable now
To see what may be done with it, to know
What should be valued in our vaunted birth,
If one may purify such vagrant blood.
Thus did I cheat them all with sophistries —
The idle crowd, that yearns the live-long day

For some new toy to wonder at. And then
I sought that thou shouldst please the king, and charm
His cares away with music. Fruitfully
That seed has prospered, for thou art to-day
His friend and comforter ; his secret heart
Admits thee as a daughter.

Valeria.
                              Do you think
His pride is dead ?

The Prince.
                      White hairs have dulled the fire
That burned so hot in youth. His mind begins
To doubt the old priority of rank.
And he will yield — there is a surer reason.
When first this cloud of war rose threatening
He summoned me, and to my sword entrusted
The safety of the state, and said to me :
Perchance these eyes may never see thee more,
My son, my child. Our case is desperate ;
Fierce ruin hangs about thy steps, and thou
Mayst scarce avoid her clutches. Shouldst thou fail,
Then all is gone but death — they are too strong,
These enemies of mine. And then we talked
Of arms and stratagems, debating chances
Through hopeless hours, till at the dawn a path
Seemed opening dimly, blind and overhung
With briers and barriers, yet that led perchance

48

To light and victory! And I shouted loud,
Crying: We 'll strike them yet — despair not yet!
Hold but a tight rein at the capital,
And by St. Michael's sword, I 'll punish them!
And as he rose, all flashing o'er with joy,
A thought sprang to my heart, and from my lips:
Give me one promise, sire, and I will win
Though all the stones were enemies! — Ask then
My crown itself! he said. Nay, sire, not that.
If I bring back the glory of our house,
The safety of the kingdom, let me have
The woman whom I love to be my wife.
The king laughed in his overflow of hope.
Thou lov'st then, Andrea? By my soul, I thought
Thy heart free as a nun's! Well, thou shouldst
        have her
Were she a goddess! So, Valeria,
The king has given his pledge, and thou —

Valeria.

And I?

The Prince.

I cast my love and power before thy feet,
My fame, the crown I shall inherit — all.
Wilt thou not take them?

Valeria.

Yes.

49

The Prince.
                              By all the saints!
Thou shalt be happy as the golden dawn!
And I will win thee kingdoms, till thy crown
Shall fit thy queenliness.   Great deeds become
As easy of achievement as a dance,
Now thou art mine forever.

Valeria.
                              I thank my lord
That he has sued for what his power might take.

The Prince.
I would not wed thee without wooing, love ;
Nor speak thy name into the public ear
Without a word to thee.   It was to say it
I rode these leagues to-night, and now again
Must ride them, for the ruthless hours lead on
Close to the morn.   To-morrow, when I come
With banners and with music, be thou near
All white, where I may see thee first.   And now
Farewell !
                    Valeria.
I will remember.

The Prince.
                              O my love,
I leave my heart upon this shrine forever,
And all my life shall be an orison.

                    [He kisses her hand.   Exit the Prince.]

Valeria.

Ah, God! this tumult in my blood and brain
Will cool up there where he has called me.   There,
Enthroned with him beyond desire, my soul
Shall rest at last — shall be at peace, at peace!
Afar from him — that other, and his eyes,
That rob me of my soul!   What words he said!
There's something in thy soul love must beware.
God keep me free of love!   God keep me free!
Me or the grave.   What deadly fear is this?
Oh, it is chill, 't is cold.   Valeria!
Alas! what hast thou done, Valeria!

[She sinks to the ground, covering her face with her hands.]

[*Curtain.*]

ACT II

ACT II

SCENE.—A spacious hall in the palace. Several ladies of the court discovered, including Tora, Piera, and Olivia.

Piera.

Faith, I am glad this weary war is over.
The court has been as full of merriment
As yonder austere convent during Lent.
I'd rather be a nun, and fast and faint,
Than play the hypocrite with mirth.

Tora.

Alas!
Piera has been lonely. When the prince
Brings back our troop of fighting friends to-day
The old sweet atmosphere of compliment
Will bring the roses to her cheeks again.

Piera.

If not, I'll hie me to the convent straight,
Where pallor is becoming.

55

Tora.

If the king
Had let us live under the cloud of war
We could have hugged our griefs with much content.
But no — he would have revels ; all the court
Must wear the laughing mask of peace, and so
What wonder if we sighed behind it ?

Piera.

None !
How can a dozen ladies cheer a court
With but a man or two to gladden them,
And those in love ?

Olivia.

This girl Valeria
Affects the bearing of a queen.

Tora.

In truth
She has it.   Doubtless she amuses you —
A stranger !

Piera.

Is she not a queen indeed,
Now that our noblest knight is at her feet ?

Olivia.

Queen of a day !   The high-born Florimond
Will not long drag his honor in the dust
Her arrogance would blind you with.

Piera.

For me,

She doth amuse me.   I profess to be
A seeker after truth, and she reveals
The worthlessness of ancestry.   I think
Were she a daughter of the Antonines
She could not walk more proudly, nor indulge
A loftier ambition.

Tora.

Did you note
How her mask vanished from the motley crowd
That vainly broke the shadowy garden's hush
Seeking Count Florimond last night — the truant?

[Enter Florimond.]

Florimond.

What lips, too sweet for aught but honeyed words,
Blend with their dulcet sounding of my name
A cruel epithet?

Piera.

My lord, what tongue,
Too lightly set to wag for truth alone,
Dares to deny the epithet?

Florimond.

A truant
Flees from the weary business of the hour
To chase bright-wingéd pleasure.   I can be

57

No truant, for my hour of banishment
From the despotic kingdom of your wit
Was spent in grave discourse. ·

Piera.

And yet 't is rumored
The wittiest despot in our crowd of masks
Found the deserter whom we sought in vain,
All in despite of darkness, and beguiled
His grave discourse.

Florimond.

Think you the woman lives
Who could discover what you fail to find?

Piera.

Your heart, my lord? The task is difficult,
The guerdon light, and yet the gossips say
One has succeeded.

Florimond.

I must doubt your wit
If you believe the gossips.

Tora.

They alone
Have not convinced us. Listen, all of you,
And judge him. When this day, so golden now,
Had slept away an hour or two in darkness,

And flaring revels flickered to their death,
I left the palace, hot with eagerness
To find a precious jewel I had lost.
I and my woman, in whose hand a torch
Sputtered its petty protest to the night,
Searched all the grassy coverts, peering deep
Down shadowy tangles I had clambered through
In the wild search for the deserter there.
When lo ! beside the thickest copse of all
A heap of star-beams lay before our feet,
Like pale flowers, new-caparisoned in dew,
And when we bent inquiringly the torch
It showed Valeria.   Prone upon the ground,
Her hands clasped high above the lifeless face
That kissed the soft caressing turf, she lay —
As though at last the orphan waif had found
A mother's greeting, and the loving earth
Had claimed her child.

Florimond.
But you revived her ?

Tora.

Long

The soul refused to greet us from her eyes,
But we despaired not, and at last it came ;
And she arose and leaning wearily
Trailed with us to the palace.

Florimond.

Did she speak ?

Tora.

Your name was on her lips and, linked with it,
Wild, unintelligible mutterings.

Piera.

Now will you still deny the interview ?

Florimond.

Nay, if you would infer sweet hours of talk
Each time a lovely lady speaks my name
My time must all be yours.

Piera.

I think it will,
For you are placed so high in my disdain
My tongue can never tell it oft enough.

Florimond.

Disdain shall have my thanks for keeping me
Fresh in your mind.   I humbly beg your grace,
Your patient, whom the perfume of sweet thoughts
Saddened to swooning — has her soul revived ?
Why comes she not ?

Tora.

She could not sleep, my lord.
This morn her cheeks are hot, and in her eyes
A sunken fire is glowing.

Florimond.

Will she come
To view the pageant?

Tora.

Though the burning fingers
Of countless fevers clutch her, she will come.
Such was her answer when I counseled rest.

Piera.

You counseled rest — to her! O lady mine,
Talk to the torrent — waste not such advice
Upon Valeria!

Florimond.

Where are your festal robes,
My tardy maids? The banners of the prince
Will crown the hill ere you are half bedecked
To grace his triumph.

Tora.

He dismisses us —
Come, let us go.

Piera.

And show this splendid count,
Whose toilet has been building since the dawn,
How swiftly they can dress who have no need
Of art and artifice.

Florimond.

Nay — who have made them slaves,
To drive the car of beauty over us.

[Exeunt all but Florimond.]

I fear my soul was dead or mad last night.
What eyes she has to witch away the world,
Make memory a void, and thought a wind
Blown from eternity to bear afar
Earth's frail illusions! Now the day grows strong
And drives away the clinging mists of night
That blinded me. I will arouse my soul,
That, lulled by perfumes, sleeps upon its task.
I will delay the triumph of my love —
Or plan it otherwise. I will prepare
And strike this blow. Three zealous months would
    do it.
Ah! 't is the curse of such a double life,
A man may lose himself in what he seems,
And be the thing he acts! I have grown dull —
The cardinal was right. The Vancua blood
Flows pale and turgid in me. Day by day
I linger here, nursing a fond pretense

Of gradual achievement, trying to forge
Great deeds with fires unlit.   Have I no strength
Even to resolve ?   Must fate supply the torch
I dare not light ?

              Faugh ! what a throng of thoughts
Comes questioning !   Away with them !

[The King's Guards approach and range themselves.   Enter the King
and Liperata.   Florimond kneels and kisses the King's hand.]

                         Alas!
In my friend's glory I shall have no share —
Would I had fought with him !

The King.
              Is all prepared ?

Florimond.
As ready as our hearts, sire.

The King.
              Will 't go well?

Florimond.
The pageant will be royal as the deed.
The town is swarming at the gates ; the hill
Is one continuous festival, and soon
Its summit will be crowned with banners, and
The waving plumes of heroes.

The King.

Hasten, then !
I envy much the doer of great deeds,
And yet thy part is dearer to my soul,
Who shalt be first to crown him with our praise.
I pray thee, weave not all the garland there
On the hill's summit.   Spare a leaf or two
To give our greeting freshness.

Florimond.

Sire, my heart
Is longing for my friend, and when once more
My hand clasps his I shall forget to hail
The prince and victor.

The King.

Leave that to the cheers
Of the rejoicing people.   Now go forth —
The glad throng waits.

Florimond.

Ah, sire, permit me now,
On this great day that makes your power immortal,
Once to salute my king, whose generous soul
Would give his heir the glory.

The King.

He will make
A king worth dynasties of such as I,
And you will live to know it.

Florimond.

I shall lose
The richest treasure of my memory first.

[He kisses the King's hand.   Exit Florimond.]

The King.

Such friends are better than dead enemies,
Whose blood enriches harvests of revenge.
Do you not think so?

Liperata.

Do not ask me, sire.
I am haunted by a shadowy distrust
Of his assiduous loyalty.

The King.

Your reason?

Liperata.

I cannot tell — I have none.   Yet of old
The chieftains of the house of Vancua
Could not so easily forget.

The King.

Of old
The Vancuas were valiant enemies,
Fierce in their hatred, swift in their revenge.
For centuries their stainless honor shone
Pure as an altar flame not once obscured

By the foul vapor of hypocrisy.
And when at last their greatness sank in blood
And night and ruin fell about their house,
I saved this youth from the impending death
That such a heritage of honesty
Might fortify me in the people's love.
Had Florimond defied me, had he spurned
My clemency, I should have recognized
The wild ancestral wilfulness; but since
He could forgive the iron hand that struck
Great blows in a great cause, that crushed their factions
To make a nation strong, and bring again
Union and power to threatened Italy —
I must believe him true, for in his blood
There is no taint of falsehood.

Liperata.

      Yet they say
His mother was a Florentine.   New times
Beget new crimes.   To-day in Italy
Traitors are thick as fig-trees.

The King.

      Have no fear.
Were he a traitor he had struck before —
Now 't is too late.   We are too strong to-day
To fear a world of foes.

Liperata.

Your majesty
Has verily the seat of Jove to-day.
Long may you hold the thunder in your hands
And late bequeath it to your dauntless son!

The King.

It is of him I dream by day and night.
He will bring back what Italy has lost.
His mother's soul shines forth in him again,
Loving and conquering.   Do you believe
That she is glad with us?

Liperata.

Can death kill love?
Where is your faith?

The King.

It faints with longing.

Liperata.

Nay,
You should not falter.   You have walked with angels —
Pure Love and sacred Sorrow.   You are blest.

[Enter, sumptuously attired, Tora, Piera, and ladies of the court.]

The King.

Hail to our rainbow-herald!   Come, what news?

Tora.

The prince is almost at the palace gates,
So pressed by loving throngs he scarce can move.

The King.

They know not our impatience.

[The King sits upon his throne. Tora advances to Liperata.]

Tora.

O my mother,
How blessed is this day! The sun climbs high,
And o'er the arid autumn of the fields
Our hero-prince comes glowing from the war!
At last the hour has come.

[Enter Cardinal Ortus and train.]

The King.

Most noble guests,
This morn to you be gracious as to me!
My bravest steeds are yours, lord cardinal,
For the long march this morning.

Cardinal.

Sire, my age
Sits not so lightly on a horse's back
As did my youth. If, then, your majesty
Will grant me but one window in the tower,

68

A friend or two from these my followers,
Their eyes will show me all, and from afar
The noise will fade to music.

The King.
Be it so —
If you desire such kindless entertainment
Through all our joy.

[Enter Valeria, in white, bearing a lute.]

Behold Valeria !
They told me she was ill, but here I see
A face all roses, starred with eyes all fire.

Valeria.
My brain was hot until the morning, sire ;
But such frail humors wait upon the will,
And mine has banished them.

The King.
'T was bravely done.

Cardinal.
The bird of song hath dipped her gaudy plumes
In the white sea-foam.

The King.
May the nereids
Have had no power to filch away her voice !

69

Valeria.

Alas! your majesty has never heard
A sea-maid's song across the waning tide,
Else would you know she need not envy me
My mortal music.

Cardinal.

You have heard it then ?

Valeria.

Oft when my soul was young, and dwelling close
With things invisible; and when the sea,
Father of music, rolled his endless tune
About mine ears.

The King.

Now let us hear her song
As you remember it.

Valeria.

I saw her rise
Star-crowned from out the sea, and snowy waves
Gemmed her bright hair with foam. Then like a bell
Rung in deep waters came her voice to me.

[*She sings.*]
The great birds beat the friendless air
    And spread their white wings wide.
The sinewy sea upholdeth me ;
    Couched softly on the tide,
The foamy winds my coursers are,
    And dauntlessly I ride.

All day the circling sun doth sweep
  His wealth along the sea;
The stars all night pursue his flight
  From bondage never free.
Yet night and day, awake, asleep,
  The ocean guardeth me.

When afar, by the turbulent winds upblown,
  Big seas pile black on high,
And the waters race to their fierce embrace
  Under a sightless sky —
In the depths whither exiled peace has flown
  I wait for the storm to die.

Oh, come hither! come over the ocean to me,
  Ye weary slaves ashore!
On his throbbing breast ye shall softly rest,
  Or, prone on the wreathéd floor,
Rapt in dreams of peace, from the mad world free,
  Ye shall toil and weep no more!

Piera.

If such a song came o'er the waves to me
I would obey and drown me.

Valeria.

                    Many a wretch,
Lured by that voice, lies stark beneath the waves.

The King.

Pray heaven we hear it not!

Valeria.
Men wholly wise
Or wholly happy never hear it, sire.

The King.
Hush ! do you hear that sound ?

Voices. [Without.]
They come ! they come !

[Clattering sounds are heard far down the distant corridor. As they
grow louder the voices of women commence this song :]

O maids, weave garlands for the dance —
    The war is done !
Pluck laurel for the conquering lance —
    The fight is won !
Come singing through the city's gate ;
Beyond, the conquering flag of state
    Gleams in the sun.

Your lords and lovers come again
  . You sent with tears.
Come dance and sing, for all in vain
    Were sighs and fears.
Come dance, for down the hill they come
To sound of fife and tap of drum —
    Rouse heaven with cheers !

Weave laurel for the victors there,
    And sing their praise ;
And, maids, if some come not to wear
    Your crown of bays,

Faint not, but dance! Unfurl on high
The flag for which they dared to die,
And pæans raise!

[While singing, the troop of maidens slowly enters, rhythmically
dancing as they sing, and scattering flowers. Then come the
King's councilors and ecclesiastical dignitaries in robes of
office. The Prince's body-guard enters next, whereupon the
King rises from his throne. During the singing all those of the
court have been visibly moved, some much excited, a few
women weeping. Valeria especially is absorbed as in a
dream, and unconsciously her body sways with the dance and
her lips move with the song. After the body-guard come the
youthful cavalcade who had gone with Florimond to meet the
Prince; and lastly Florimond leads in Prince Andrea himself,
followed by his chief officers, among them being Count Leone.
As Valeria sees Florimond she shrinks back with a shudder,
and covers her face with her hands. But the next instant she
draws herself proudly up and meets his eye in a long gaze,
while the King descends the steps from the throne, and the
Prince hastens to kneel at his feet.]

The King.

Rise—to my heart, and may the frown of fate
Part us no more! If I were rich in speech
My praise should set thy name among the stars,
My son!

The Prince.
At last I feel thy blood in me.

The King.

My conqueror!

The Prince.
Thine enemies', my lord.

73

Where are they ?

The Prince.

Sire, thou hast none.   Read the proof
Here, in this treaty.

[The King takes the parchment, and the two read and converse together in an undertone.   In the mean time Andrea's officers seek
out their wives and friends in the throng.]

Liperata.

Joy is queen again!
Conquerors, were your pathway paved with gems
'T were yet unworthy.   All our hearts' delight
No pageantry can tell.

Tora.

We thank you all,
And for your scars we weep.   Signor, 't was you
Who led them by the woody mountain-pass
To strike the enemy's heart.   We heard the tale.
Ah, Count Leone, have you sheathed your sword
To whet your tongue again ?

Leone.

My lady, no;
I crown you victor in the war of words
And dare contend no more.

74

Tora.

Brave deeds alone
Beget such modesty.   My noble lord,
Your race is rich in glory—and your brother,
Where is he ?

Agnolo.

Dead, my lady.

Tora.

Nay, his name
Will live when we are dead.   'T is well with him.
Alas ! I know a maid will weep for this —
Bear her the tidings gently.

Valeria.

[To three or four gentlemen who have sought her out.]

Now may the world be merry once again.
Such funeral revels we have held, my lords—
With terror at the gates, and fierce despair
Luring the enemy hither.

A Gentleman.

Had they come,
You need but sing to charm their hate away
And make them slaves.

Valeria.

I 'll sing no more, my lords ;
Then will you let me brood in solitude,
Until, aweary of the faithless world,

I drag my lone soul to a nunnery
And tune my harp for heaven.

Florimond.

Sing no more—
Your speech alone is tuneful. Speak no more—
There 's music in your eyes. Be blind and dumb,
And still the spirit of melodious sounds
Will be your herald.

Valeria.

And when I shall die
Music will perish with me. Ah, my lords,
Forgive this courtier! In the fire of war
You must have purged your souls of flattery—
Teach him how easy 't is to speak the truth.
What are you seeking, Count Leone? Grant me
But half a word.

Leone.

I knew a lady once—
Tell me, I pray you, has she died of grief?

Valeria.

'T is but a leaden conscience drags her from you.
Question her well, my lord, and trust her little —
If this is she.

[Moving aside, she reveals Piera, who has been hiding from Leone,
and now comes forward smiling.]

Leone.

Say thou hast kept the faith,
Most noble lady.

Piera.

Do not praise me for it.
If I remember you 't is but because
No rivals sued, my lord.

Leone.

I know full well
You were half dead with grieving, and your face
Betrays the fasts and vigils, and the tears
You spent for me.

Piera.

If I am thin, the cause
Is revelry, for I assure your worship
We have been merry far into the night.
We know how jauntily the world would spin
Were naught but women in it.

Leone.

And we men
Dreamed you were pining for us, and forbore
To woo the golden damsels of the north
In pity for you.

Piera.

Constancy is made
Of false compassion, then.

Leone.

Nobler than yours,

Which dares not face a tempter.

Piera.

You forget —

I never promised constancy.

Leone.

I know

You wept upon me with a storm of sighs
The day we parted.

Piera.

Strange I should have feared,

Who know you are so dear in your own love
That the most tempting danger ne'er could lure
Your feet from safety !

Leone.

If my sword was cold

'T was for your sake who could not live without me.

Piera.

The brave new chivalry !   Of old a knight
Offered great deeds like jewels to his love,
Or fell to prove him worthy of her tears.

Leone.

What if a knight, whose arm would strive in vain
To add a splendor to his lady's name,

Yet felt the sweet infusion of her soul
Urging him on to glory, and essayed
To be not all ignoble, would she hold
His striving worthy the divine reward?

Piera.

I am not worthy such a knight, my lord.
Go ask some nobler lady.

Leone.

I should seek her
Through all the world in vain.

The King. [To the Prince.]

We are safe again!
Once more we clutch care by the throat, and smooth
The frowning brow of fate.   My Andrea,
Thy father is thy debtor for his crown;
To the last word thou hast fulfilled thy promise.

The Prince.

And thine, my father?

The King.

I do not forget.
Hast thou considered well?

The Prince.

That hope has been
The torch that led me on.

The King.

And she is here —

The lady whom thou lov'st ?

The Prince.

Ah! suffer me

With her to kneel before thee!

The King.

No — not yet.

The world must be our witness to the bond —

So shall we not escape, though all go ill.

[The King ascends and stands in front of the throne, followed by the
Prince, who takes his position just below him.]

My countrymen! — you whose intrepid souls

Have borne our honor up the steeps of war,

And you who from afar with hearts aflame

Have watched their fierce ascent and cheered them on,

Loosing the leash of treasure ; you as well,

Mothers and wives of heroes, maidens pure,

Whose high hearts wept the night away in prayers

Till the glad dawn revealed a smiling heaven —

Well have you served the state! The insolent foe

Crawls at your feet, and on the heights of fame,

Caressed by skyey breezes, far above

The reach of envious clouds, impregnable,

Your flag floats, streaming forth its hues of dawn,

Lit by the sun of glory. For your toil,

Triumphant now, we thank you.   For your wounds,
Your losses, and your woes a weeping land
Uplifts her arms in blessing, and her praise,
Smiling through tears, crowns each devoted head
With immortality.   May tender Peace
Dwell on your hearths forever!   Joyous days
Be your reward, and softly sunny age,
Mellowed by mighty memories!

                        To one,
Your leader in the brotherhood of arms,
First in our pride and dearest in our love,
We grant a special boon.   Prince Andrea
Claims as the promised prize of victory
The lady of his love to be his wife.
To him, who from the daughters of great kings
May choose his spouse, we grant the privilege
Of marriage with the lowliest, if such
Be his desire.   Yet we beseech his youth
That no hot-blooded passion may obscure
His duty to the state, which asks of him
A queen of race heroic, fit to be
The mother of great sons.

The Prince.

                    Sire, I am come
From battle, and the iron robes of war
Still cling about me.   At my side still hangs
The sword I wielded for my country's right.

Think you unholy fires could e'er survive
The red rain of that quenching? In my love
I am still a patriot, and the maid I choose,
Were she descended from a race of kings,
And dowered with states for jewels, could not bring
A soul more royal nor a richer store
Of queenly treasures.   With most humble hope
I beg the purest thing of all the earth
To stoop to such a battered warrior
And teach him how to reign.

[He kneels to Valeria.]

Valeria.

Ah, not to me!

You shame me to the soul.

The King.

Alas! my son—

Come back to me, my son!

The Prince.

Will you be false?

I lean upon your promise and your love.

The King.

And in the name of love I bid you pause.

The Prince.

When the long race is close upon the goal
You bid the winner pause!   Recall such folly!

82

The King.

The goal you seek is but a veering vane,
The prize as volatile as air is.

Valeria.

Sire,

Even you shall not insult me.

The Prince.

Do not speak;

Trust to my love for all.

Valeria.

Most noble prince,
This blessing of your love would make me rich;
But if the king doth scorn my empty hands
And meager lineage, I repay his scorn.
Great is he in the empire of the sword —
In the pure realm of art my ancestors
Were kings when his were bandits. On my soul
I will not wed on sufferance. Give me back
The wild free life you stole me from, my lord.
Then was I empress of the world. My mind
Was sister to great poets, and my soul
Sang like the harp of God, and was at peace.

The King.

It is the truth — she is a thing afar.
Our kingdom is not hers, nor is she fit
To bear the bonds of earthly sovereignty.

My son, the colors of the dawn are fair;
But weave a mantle of the morning cloud
And it will chill thee.   Let my love once more
Bid thee beware.

Valeria.

I, too, entreat my lord
Not to enforce this whim.   Ah, let me go!

The Prince.

Dost thou forget?—Sire, have I ever changed?

The King.

Then must this be?

The Prince.

Ay, by my mother's soul.

The King.

Then ring the bells — bid the great host advance,
And set beside the conqueror's coal-black steed
A snow-white palfrey for his fair betrothed.
And let the heralds to the world proclaim
The hero and the maid who one week hence
Shall be his bride.

Tora.

Mother, must we ride too?

Liperata.

With heavy hearts, my child.

Tora.

I know a journey
More easy for the soul.   God! let me take it!

The King. [To Valeria.]
Come hither, child.

[Valeria, led by the Prince, approaches and kneels before him.]

Be true, as she was true!
Be steadfast.   Seek for peace within thy soul —
It will not meet thee in the arms of power.
Trust not the sylvan spirit of unrest
That calls thee from the past.   Thy golden hour
Is fled.   No more canst thou be Nature's guest,
For Life has beckoned to thee, and has poured
Her riches in thy lap, and whispered thee
Her luring mysteries.   Remember not,
Seek not, but walk straight on in thankfulness,
Trusting thy joy to God.   So shalt thou be
Queen of thy soul, that long has idly roved
The slave of every wind.   So shall thy reign
Make brave men strong.

Valeria.

O sire, I have been rash,
But not ungrateful.   In this embassy
From my domain to yours my heart shall bear
The treasures of art's kingdom for a dower,
But my allegiance is to yours forever.

The Prince.

Heaven make me worthy of thee!

Valeria.

Mock me not!
I know not why thou lov'st me.

The Prince.

Happy years
Shall prove my constancy.

[At the King's command above — "Bid the great host advance"
—the crowd begins to file out, led by the soldiers and dancing
maidens, who softly take up their old refrain. Then the officers
and people·of the court leave more informally to mount and
form outside, followed by Liperata and Tora, and then by the
Prince and Valeria. During the gradual exit the following
scene occurs at the front of the stage.]

Florimond. [Turning to follow — aside.]

Ambitious puppet!
She 'll wish her soul in hell ere all is done.

The King.

Cardinal, I am loath to leave you. Count,
Attend our noble guest, and from the tower
Show him the spectacle.

Florimond.

One word, my king.
The prince has stolen the jewel of my heart —

I cannot see him wear it. Let me go!
Let me not sour his joy with jealous thoughts.
The world is wide to roam in, and afar
My soul shall find content. Deny me not
A little time to purge away this grief
That stains my friendship with disloyalty.

The King.
Is love so grave a thing to you as well?
Yes—you shall have the passports. See the world,
And bring us news of it.

Florimond.
                        When I return
A heart reborn to freedom and true faith
Shall thank you fitly.

[Exit the King and train; and, at a sign from Florimond, the
followers of the Cardinal.]
                        I am yours. This hour
My soul is turned to steel.

Cardinal.
                        A Vancua!

Florimond.
I shall not stand again upon this ground
Till I can throttle them. We will go hence—
To-morrow be it! He has granted me

Arms for his ruin.   From the distant hills
Freedom shall call her forces.   When these tyrants
Walk most securely under azure skies
A storm shall burst upon them, and my hand
Shall hurl the thunderbolt against their throne.

Cardinal.

I hear thy father's voice in thine again.
Swift be the blessèd march of liberty!

[*Curtain.*]

ACT III

ACT III

[SCENE.—The antechamber of the Princess Valeria. Enter the Captain of the King's Guards with Florimond, who is soiled and stained with travel. Three months elapse between Acts II. and III.]

Captain.

You are too bold, my lord.

Florimond.

What should I fear?
This is a house of bats. The rising sun
But strikes them blind.

Captain.

The sun has not yet risen,
And they are on the watch. Why did you come
When any messenger would do as well?

Florimond.

To be of use, Rinaldo. Do not fret.
I have seen the king and sugared him with words
Till his soul soaks in sweet content. Besides,

91

He is a phantom; who would touch me now
At his command?

Captain.
Not I, my lord.   And yet
Are we prepared for disobedience?

Florimond.
To the last banner.   Not a man but knows
His part in the play, and strains his eager ear
To catch the first glad call of liberty.

Captain.
And when will she awake?

Florimond.
To-morrow night.
I come to give the signal.

Captain.
God be thanked!
'T is worth a score of years of servitude
To feel the breath of freedom once again.

Florimond.
To-morrow is our blesséd patron's feast,
And Count Leone's wedding-day as well.

The city will be thronged, and with the crowd,
Like a fleet shadow at the heels of joy,
Our people will assemble; and at night,
When revels have grown drunk, one word from me
Will end this farce with fire.

Captain.

But are you sure
The citizens are ours? Prince Andrea
Has won them by the very candor of
His tyrannous force.

Florimond.

I will dispose of him —
He will not vex us when the moment comes.
And for the citizens, my name alone
Has been their talisman for centuries.
What is this prince that he should charm away
A nation's soul? A Vancua need but whistle
To wake the mighty goddess slumbering here,
Her head upon our hills. When she doth rise
The past will shine again deep in her eyes —
And woe to those who see the lightnings there!

Captain.

I vowed to give my slave-born children back
The heritage we lost. My hand is yours —
For life or death.

93

Florimond. [Hearing footsteps without.]

The count was long my friend,
His bride too long my enemy — and yet
I think she loved me well, save with her tongue.

[Enter Tora and Piera.]

Piera.

The Count of Vancua! Is he still alive,
And talking still?

Florimond.

Close to his end, my lady.
He lingers but a day — his tongue will rot
When you are married.

Tora.

Welcome, truant friend.
How we have longed for you!

Florimond.

To-morrow's bride
Desired my pardon for past cruelty?

Piera.

Ah, no! Your thanks for many a priceless truth.

Florimond.

You have them — you shall have your will to-day,
To the last sting. But I beseech your grace

For this unworthy livery.   The slave
Of two such lovely ladies lives in heaven —
No stains of earth should soil him.   Let me go;
I am not fit to kiss a lady's hand,
White as the rapture we invoke for her.

Piera.

Ah, count, if all the hapless world to-night
Might be as glad as I !   I shall rejoice
Through all my joy to see you here to-morrow.
Good-night !

Tora.

You are the capstone of our hopes.

Florimond.

More eager in your service than the king's.

[Exit Florimond.]

Tora.

'T is our last night, Piera; 't is the end.
To-night we stand together on the shore;
To-morrow comes the shining barge of gold,
Its captain at the rudder — all his soul
Deep burning in his eyes, imploring thine.
His strong arms open, and he waves afar
Over the purple ocean shot with gold,
Waves to the blessèd islands of delight,
Deep buried in the distant blue.   And thou —

Wrapt in a robe of dreams, serene, secure,
Thy soul glides on, and I am left alone.

Piera.

Thou art the dreamer, Tora. Long ago
We vowed our sisterhood, and registered
Our deathless scorn of men — dost thou remember?
And longed to prove our constancy against
The wooing of a host of suppliants. Ah!
I am forsworn — I did not know them then,
These suitors. One has turned the heavy key
That locked the secret chambers of my heart,
And lo! the day pours in, and I awake,
Who never lived before. All is more rich
Touched by this golden sun of love. The past
Transfigured is, not plundered. Thou art still
The twin star of my soul.

Tora.

Until the dawn —
What star can shine undimmed before the sun?

Piera.

Leave me not on the wings of metaphor!
The stars are older than the fiery sun
And each to other never dim. My friend,
Talk not of change. So knitted are our souls
We cannot disentangle all the past.

Tora.

Leave it to memory, in whose shadowy realm
Grant to our love a consecrated shrine,
And strew it with fresh thoughts when we are parted.

Piera.

My sister, look at me! What blight is this,
Blasting our fellowship? Is marriage then
An exile? Will the count imprison me,
Deny me friends, feed me with poisonous doubts?
Thou dost not think so! Tell me then at once
Why thou canst speak of parting.

Tora.

I must go —
God wills it — I obey.

Piera.

In God's name, where?

[Tora points to the distant convent, whose bells are even then almost
inaudibly ringing.]

Tora.

Unto a royal marriage.

Piera.

Is 't resolved?

Tora.

Three months have idled on since I resolved.

Piera.

And nothing said?

Tora.

I waited but for thee —
Thy wedding. When Leone claims his bride
The portals of the cloister will receive me.

Piera.

Hast thou no mercy on thy youth? Dost know
The penances, the vigils, and the fasts,
The bare cold days, the long entombéd nights,
The endless years stretching in vista'd gloom
Down to the grave? Oh, hast thou thought of all i

Tora.

All these are nothing. From the fires of life
My soul has risen to heaven. I am at peace.

Piera.

Ah, life is glorious — action, love, the world
To rove in, laden with beauty and delight.

Tora.

Sweet be its songs to thee, its loveliest flowers
Fall in thy lap! For thee and thy content
One will be praying always.

Piera.

Say no more.
Thy soul is far away — I cannot hear.

But in my cup of joy salt tears are falling,
And all my bridal robes are wound with black.
Tora!

Tora.

My sister!

[They embrace.]

Piera.

Is it farewell indeed?

Tora.

Not to our love.

[Enter the Princess Valeria.]

Valeria.

What! weeping, girls — my girls?
Ah, you are wise, Piera; 't is with tears
A maid should think of marriage.

Piera.

Then am I
Most false to maidenhood, for these my tears
Fall on another altar.

Valeria.

Are you happy?

Piera.

In all my thoughts of the sweet time to come
As glad as any queen — so please your highness.

Valeria.

She does not know. [Aside.] If I could bless you now
I would importune death to bear you hence.

Piera.

What fearful thought is this?

Valeria.

Ah, child, sweet child —

Piera.

Nay, madam, take the measure of our years
And mine are more than yours.

Valeria.

Oh, I am old —
Old as the Apennines!   My childhood lies
Deep at their base — too deep for memory,
And icy age sits throned upon my brow.
I ask you, child, what fate could be more sweet
Than death in love's first ecstasy?

Piera.

Long life
Spent in love's service.

Valeria.

Be it so to you!
Why do you weep if all is well with you?

Tora.

Madam, for me ; my choice is nearer yours,
Since nearer death than life. The world and I
To-morrow shall be parted.

Valeria. [Bowing reverently.]
Pray for me
When you are vowed to God.

Tora.
For you, great princess ?
Alas ! what more can you demand of God ?

Valeria.

Such wisdom and such happiness as yours —
Strength to renounce ; for in that bitter word
Wisdom and joy clasp hands in ecstasy.

Tora.

You chose to read another. Love and power
Sing in your ears, and will you envy me
The one white thought God whispers to my soul?
Ah, leave me that ! God knows you have enough
To be content.

Valeria.

Ah yes! to me the world,
And heaven to thee. To have or to renounce !
Cypress and myrtle are the wreaths of joy
Life crowns her chosen with. Piera here

Shall wear the myrtle ever — all my soul
Prays heaven for that, but for the cypressed nun
No need of prayer — her I congratulate.

Tora.

I thought you rich, and do you envy me
My poverty?

Valeria.

That soul alone is rich
Who is content. What feasts can satisfy
Implacable desire? Would you be free
Feed not the monster — kill it! I, you see,
Can still philosophize, whom Fortune's wand
Has tricked to splendor and to happiness.
Still must I know what others must endure.

Piera.

Princess, you live ten thousand lives in one.
Are you not tired?

Valeria.

I cannot quite forget
The artist in my blood.

Piera.

What is an artist?

Valeria.

The mirror of all souls.

Tora.

Has such an one
Herself a soul ?   Ah, madam, you were right,
And I will pray for you.

Valeria.

Ho, this is scorn !
Go — whisper to the ocean ; lean upon
The shaggy breast of mountains ; ride afar
Over the soaring clouds ; then multiply
The narrow kingdom of your coward wit
By infinite emotions and desires,
And you shall know a little what it is
To have an artist's soul.

Tora.

May Christ in heaven
Spare me the knowledge !

Valeria.

Have no fear ! not all
His power could give it you.

Tora.

Your highness —
[Tora controls herself with an effort.]

Piera.

Nay,
Each to her happiness.   Now here am I

Content with such a lean and piteous wit
It scarce can stagger from the daily range,
Or stutter out a question to the stars.
Can you, who are so learned in ancient lore,
Tell why I ignorantly smile with fortune,
Or blindly sadden when she crosses me ?

[Enter Prince Andrea and Count Leone.]

Most noble lords, these ladies delve in vain
Deep in the elements.   Come, rescue them !

Leone.

They are content.   'T is you need rescuing.

Piera.

Ah, let me go !   This is my last of freedom —
You would not be so thievish.

Leone.

I was born
Of a most grasping temper.

The Prince.

Spare him not !
Your power is waning — strain it to the last.
My ladies, have you seen the wanderer,
Our latest wedding guest ?

Piera.

A moment since
We caught him with the travel-stains upon him,

And he was so abashed he fled away
To don his satins.

Valeria. [Aside.]

It is Florimond.

The Prince.

My heart is glad indeed ; though I, his friend,
Might well be jealous of his enemy.
Some strange, mad, sudden wish to see the world
Made him a truant from my wedding ; yet
He dares return for yours.

Leone.

'T is but revenge.
He longs to see her bowed under the yoke.

Valeria.

Count, you would jest at death.   Most noble ladies,
Your confessors await you, and we crave
No further talk to-night.

Tora. [To Piera.]

Ah !   God is good
To call me hence.

Piera.

Hush, child !

The Prince.

Leone,
The king desires your presence for a moment.

I 'll join you soon.   Sleep well to-night, fair maiden.
Leone shall awake you with a song.

[Exeunt Leone, Tora, and Piera, bowing.]

Valeria.

When did the count return ?

The Prince.

An hour ago.
I vow thou art more royal than the heir
Of fifty kings.   Who taught thee to command ?
I love to see thee queen it over them.

Valeria.

'T is not so difficult a part to play.

The Prince.

Yet once I loved thee for thy simpleness,
Thy sweet, wild freedom from the taint of courts,
That breed hypocrisy.

Valeria.   [Wearily.]

Ah ! once for that,
To-day for this, to-morrow for the other.
Pray, can you never love me for myself?

The Prince.

What means my wife ?

106

Valeria.

Oh, I am not so good,
So simple, nor so loyal as you dream.
Your will enslaves your eyes. You see in me
The image of your thought. You know me not.

The Prince.

I know your steadfast truth and gentleness.
If there is ought beside in woman's soul
Let me not know it!

Valeria.

There is much beside
You cannot catalogue by phrases thus.
We range in flowery fields, 'mid changing winds,
The skies all in an April mood for showers,
While you would prison us in nice ideas.
Ah, give your fancy wings, and try to feel
What 't is to be a woman.

The Prince. [Embracing her.]

What care I
For all the women in the world but one?
I cannot tell how deep is my content.
Fear not this weight of honors — thou couldst wear
The crown of all the Cæsars on thy brow
And not be overborne. That thou art happy
And rescued from the sloughs of circumstance

Is joy that chokes my prayers with thankfulness.
Strive always to be cheerful as thy fate;
And be not jealous if the king's affairs
Pluck me away from thee.   Even now, my sweet,
He waits me.   Strange designs must be discussed.

Valeria.

What strange designs ?

The Prince.
Lady inquisitive,
Thou wouldst not know.   Think of a song instead —
I long to hear a song when I return
After my hour of penance.

Valeria.
Wouldst thou hear
The caged lark sing ?

The Prince.
I fear thou art not well.
I 'll send to thee some people to beguile
Thy loneliness.

Valeria.
No—I am very well.
I do not fear an hour of solitude.
Go to the king.

The Prince.

First crown me with a kiss.

[He kisses her.   Exit the Prince.]

Valeria.

Oh, when he touches me, I hate him so
That I do fear myself.   What shall I do?
My God! what shall I do?   To be a wife —
What is it but to walk in mortal shame,
And see no shrine where pluméd hope may rest
And beckon to the soul!   If I could die —
Like honey from the fields of liberty
The draught of death would taste.   Oh, to be free!
To dance once more adown the blooming roads,
My soul all song!   To sleep beneath the stars,
Close to the heart of Nature, and to hear
Her whispers all alone!   To wander hence
Back to the past — to hunger, nakedness!
I cannot breathe.   I can but gnaw the chains
That link my soul to earth forevermore —
While Fate stands mocking me, and crying loud,
I have fulfilled thy dreams!   Blind fool of fortune —
Tempted by glitter, gulled by the show of power,
Tricked by ambition into slavery,
And dumb with my despair!

                 — And one has come
Whose glance will read it all, though it be hid
'Neath rosy heights of laughter, though I pile

Vast clouds of happy phrases to conceal
The burning horror at my heart.   His hand
Will touch it — he will know.

        Ah, saints in heaven !
If I could only play it to the end —
This rôle I blindly chose — and be a queen
Even over misery !

  [Enter Florimond.   Valeria rises and confronts him.]

      Why do you come
Intruding on my solitude ?

      Florimond.
      Is this
Your greeting after all the weary months ?

      Valeria.
To-morrow I will welcome you.   To-night
I crave the hour alone.

      Florimond.
      Upon my soul
I bow before you.

      Valeria.
    Count !

      Florimond.
      This royal farce —
You play it to the life.

Valeria.

What right have you
To question my commands?

Florimond.

Ah! none at all.
The man who loves you, he whose memory bears
The record of your vows — what right has he
To anything but scorn?

Valeria.

Man, have you lived
So long upon this earth, and never learned
Some pages in the book of memory
Must be erased forever?

Florimond.

Woman, woman,
Canst thou erase the pages written deep
In heart's-blood from a wound that never heals?
Hast thou forgotten all?

Valeria.

I will forget.

Florimond.

Oh, empty boast! Who can escape the past?
Not all thy tears through weary years of woe
Shall wash one word away. Why should we speak

The chatter of the court, as if my heart
Knew not each throb of thine ?   Unhappy one !
I cannot see thee suffer and be dumb.
I know what thou hast done.

Valeria.

And if you know
Why do you torture me ?   What I have done
I freely did.   I only am to blame.

Florimond.

No, not to blame.   Thy soul an eagle is,
Seeking the sun.   It is not strange at all
That eyes unwonted to the light of power
Mistook the bauble on a royal brow
For the full orb of day.   No — not to blame !
The tortures I have suffered in thy loss
Urged no reproach to thee.

Valeria.

'T is generous !
Ah ! would to God the voice within my heart
Might be as merciful !

Florimond.

Think not of that !
The past is with the dead, and like a corse
Abhorrent to the thought.   Let not thy soul
Sink in the grave with rotten memories

To taint the coming years. Art thou not brave?
Hast thou no thought beyond thine own distress?
The times are comfortless. A million souls
Are longing for deliverance, and thou —
What hast thou done?

Valeria.
                    What do I know, my lord,
Of the wide world beyond me?

Florimond.
                              Wouldst thou know?

Valeria.
I faint for knowledge.

Florimond.
                       Though its cup were red
With human blood and salt with human tears,
Still would you drink it?

Valeria.
                          To the dregs, my lord.
Think you I have no pity?

Florimond.
                          Are you still
A daughter of the people? Though you wear
Gaudy disguises, are you loyal still
To the rude blood that warms you?

Valeria.

I would give
These gauds and all I ever hoped of power
For one wild dance along the grassy fields.
All this is but the badge of slavery,
The emblem of despair. If you can see
A window in my prison, lead me there,
And let me view again the mighty world
Where I can rove no more.

Florimond.

Then come with me,
And through the window of my memory
Gaze out upon the past. What dost thou see?
A city, cradled on a tide-swept shore,
Whose infant ears heard from the clamorous surf,
From salt sea-winds and thunderous mountain gales,
But one word — liberty! And as she grew,
Bathing her strong free limbs in mighty seas,
Circling o'er broad domains her puissant arms,
That word was still the key-note of her song,
And from her lovely eyes fierce lightnings flashed
At thought of an oppressor. Year by year
And age by age her comeliness increased,
And every violent hand that dared assail
She hurled to ruin, all her soul athrill
With the fierce pride of freedom. Long she reigned,
And all her people, gladdened by her smile,

114

Wrought for her glory, till her shining hair
Was strung with diamonds, and her spotless robe
With pearls embroidered and with silks enriched,
Until in splendid modesty she stood
Peerless among the nations.   Thus she was!
Alas!   What is she now?

Valeria.

                    Ah! even as I —
Wedded to misery.

Florimond.

                    Not wedded — no,
Despoiled, shamed, outraged!   Ah, the bitter tale
They sweetened for thee.   Listen to the truth.

Valeria.

Oh, let me know it!

Florimond.

                    When this king was young
He and his tribe were exiled for their crimes —
A violent faction, who had dashed with blood
The robes of liberty.   For years they wandered
Over the face of Italy, in vain
Seeking to soothe the rigid front of justice;
While we at home basked in the noon of peace,
Busy with dreams, blind summer slumberers.
At last a cloud came thundering from the north;

A military chief—soldier of fortune—
Hung cities on his sword-belt, as a thief
Slips jewels in his pocket, till his arm
Threatened our citadel inviolate.
Then we awoke into a strange eclipse,
And, mad with fear, we called our exiles home
To fight the foreign foe.   The call rang forth
And roused them from despair.   With sword and spear
O'er hills and seas they came, and ranged their strength
Under the banner which my father bore—
The state's appointed captain.
                              But their aid
Was needless, for the threatening despot died,
And the fantastic structure of his power
Fell like a summer dream.
                              When all was safe
Within the city's walls flashed up once more
O'ershadowed memory, and the bloody past
Rose like a ghost, with hand omnipotent
Closing the clanging gates, and hurling thence
A new decree of banishment against
The gathered host of exiled wanderers.

Valeria.

Pitiless mother! could she not forgive
Her sons who came to save?

Florimond.

                    Who came to save!
Nay, to devour!   Ruin was in their hearts—

The savage hearts of traitors. To their arms
Nothing she owed, for not a sword was flushed
When death struck down the foe. Yet some abhorred
Even the suspicion of a stain, and pleaded
For their admission. Lo ! even while they prayed
Swift as a rocket sprang the signal forth,
And war was at our doors. All Italy
Was roused or cowed by the arch mischief-breeder,
And wrought for our despair, or stood agape
While the inviolate city he had sworn
To cherish and defend he stripped and plundered
Of every rag of honor.

Valeria.
'T was the king !

Florimond.
Ay, 't was the king, who should have died to save
His country from a tyrant. He it was
Who led a mob of fierce adventurers —
The cutthroats of all nations and his own —
Straight to his childhood's home, whose loveliness
Long peace had garlanded, and turned them loose
To wreak their horrid will and his revenge.

Valeria.
Oh, horrible !

Florimond.
Should I reveal it all —
The story of those days so charged with crime —
Your soul would sicken, and your heart grow old.

Valeria.

Am I not guilty too ? 'T is fit I know
The sins I have espoused.

Florimond.

Not all — not all.
One deed will be enough to prove the whole —
The death of one old man.   A gentle mind
Was his, brave and compassionate and true.
He pleaded for these outlaws, would have risked
Receiving them as brothers at the hearth
They had so wantonly profaned.
The rack was his reward; and when his soul
Seemed to have vanished from its ruthless clutch
They flung his body in the street, and mocked
Our white-lipped agony.

Valeria.

And the great God
Could watch it from his heaven !

Florimond.

Beyond — beyond
He saw the end, and planted in that deed
The seeds of retribution ; for the life
Pent in that form, torn, mangled, piteous,
Sprang to cold lips again, breathed fiery words
No mortal soul could hear and disobey.
And at the last, when death drooped over him,

He smiled, for his ancestral legacy —
The love of freedom, and the hate of wrong —
His son had vowed to vindicate — or die.

Valeria.

And you are he.

Florimond.

'T was I who made that vow.

Valeria.

And you have lived so long without revenge.

Florimond.

Revenge which will be sure must needs be slow.
The time has come.

Valeria.

The method and the means—
Tell me, I must know all.

Florimond.

Will you be strong ?

Valeria.

As strong as death.

Florimond.

Do you love liberty ?

Valeria.

I — liberty ? You who have seen me free —
You ask me that ?

Florimond.

Would you for liberty,
The freedom of a million souls enslaved,
Strike one brave blow, risk one soft luxury
Of praise or pleasure, or of peaceful days?

Valeria.

I would give all!   What can she ask of me
I would not proudly grant?

Florimond.
                          Then her demand
Will be your law?

                  Valeria.
                  I swear it.   Would to God
That I could free the world!

                          Florimond.
                          This guilty race
Must die.
                  Valeria.
          And is the other guilty too—
My husband?

                  Florimond.
                  When the streets ran red with blood,
Almost a child he stood beside his father
Cheering and urging on the murderous work—
A frenzied fiend of impious energy.

In him the crimes of future years are lodged.
And shall he live ?   You who have felt the bonds,
Can aught but death level his jagged will ?

Valeria.

My soul is on the rack beneath it, yet
There seems in him a kind of innocence —
As who should stroke a bird that longs to fly,
And dream it loves the touch.

Florimond.

There lies the peril.
Craft we can meet, but such simplicity
Is like a gag choking our weary groans
Till the world deems our silence happiness.
His soul breathes incense as its natural air.
The state is on the rack, yet in his mind
She rests upon a bed of violets,
Dreaming of naught but love and gratitude.
Himself is in his eye, and all the world
Is but his shadow.   He is the enemy.
When he is dead freedom will rise again
Fearless and strong.   She does not dread the king.

Valeria.

How shall he die ?

Florimond.

Dear lady, 't is to you
The stricken city calls.   Insulted justice

Arms you for her revenge.   I have a weapon,
Petty yet potent.

[He drops a pellet into a cup on the table, and fills it with wine
from a vessel standing near.]

When the prince comes back
Give him this golden wine.   He will not feel it.
Pain will not touch nor frenzy torture him,
And death will give no sign for many hours;
Yet when this time to-morrow shall have rung
He will exist no more.

Valeria.
—Exist no more—
There is no other way—it must be done?

Florimond.
For God and liberty.

Valeria.
And when 't is done
Will all be over?

Florimond.
The people are in arms,
And we will fight for it.   To-morrow night
The city shall be free.

Valeria.
Have they no friends—
They who were once so strong?   Was he not crowned
By suffrage of the people?

Florimond.

You have heard it —
Their treacherous boast! Perchance there was a day
When fear went mad, and bought security
With shame. The knife was at the city's throat,
But far away the fields were clad in blue —
The future smiled redemption, and she looked,
And could not die. But she remembers well,
And for the past to-morrow will atone.

Valeria.

And we shall all be free forevermore.

Florimond.

Sweet is the sacred wrath of Liberty —
Lovely her flaming eyes! But sweeter far
Her tenderness for those who serve her well.
The noblest sons of time have writ their names
In stars about her brow, and with them now
Thine own will shine forever.

Valeria.

I could die
To be enshrined in the world's love forever.
I would fear nothing, suffer everything.

Florimond.

I know it, and I trust thee.

[Enter Prince Andrea, a bloody sword in his hand.]

123

The Prince.

He is dead —

The slanderer !

Valeria.

What means this bloody sword?

The Prince.

He slandered thee, and so I struck him dead.

Valeria.

Who slandered me ?

The Prince.

Leone.

Valeria.

And you killed him ?

The Prince.

Listen ! he said you were conspiring here —
My wife, my friend ! — conspiring for my death.
'T is false ! and he is dead.

He dared to say it —
No man can whisper such a calumny
And stand against my sword ! — he told me there
The wine was poisoned — 't is a damnéd lie !

[He suddenly seizes the cup. Valeria makes a motion to arrest him, but he drains it instantly.]

Now is the slander dead, and gone to hell !

[Valeria falls to the ground, and embraces his feet.]

Valeria.

My husband!

The Prince.

Oh, my wife! that he should say it!
What could I do but kill him?

[*Curtain.*]

ACT IV

ACT IV

Agnolo.

Who is the assassin ?

Filippo.

                    Who can name him now ?
The Count Leone had no enemies.

Agnolo.

I loved him ! I would give this my right hand
To know the dastard who has struck him down.
The awful days are come again, when hate
Hides in a dirk and dares not wield a sword ;
When every friend may be an enemy,
And every cup a lurking-place for death.

Filippo.

Ah, nevermore ! The king will know the truth
And punish, as of old. 'T was I who told him —
I know it by the fury in his eyes.

Agnolo.

I told the unhappy lady who should be
His bride to-day.   I roused her from her sleep,
And told her they had found her lover dead,
Wishing that I were buried with my news.

Filippo.

Poor lady, did she weep ?

Agnolo.

              Her eyes were dry,
Her face white as a shroud.   She said no word,
But followed to his bier, where now she clings
Moaning and fondling him.   It maddens me !

Filippo.

Be calm, and trust the king.   High in the state
Was the dead count, Prince Andrea's cherished friend.
His death will be avenged.

Agnolo.

             Look where she comes !
That face of hers will haunt me in my dreams.
Come — let us go.

[Exeunt Agnolo and Filippo.   Enter Tora and Piera, the latter
passive in her friend's hands.]

Tora.

          Piera, speak to me !
Is there no comfort in the tears of God
That thou shouldst be so still ?

Piera.

There's naught to say.

Tora.

There's death to mourn, justice to be invoked.

Piera.

Justice! How can they give me justice now,
When he is dead?

Tora.

Against the coward hand
That murdered him wilt thou not cry aloud?
[Aside.] My brain is branded with a name; mine eyes
Can see naught else—it is Valeria!
Somewhere—I know not how—her finger lies
Under this mischief; I would stake my soul,
So sure am I! [To Piera.] Shall the assassin live?

Piera.

If they could steep his impious soul in blood
Would that restore my husband to my arms?
There is no justice in the courts of heaven
Or he would not have died.

Tora.

Poor soul of woman!
Wilt thou assail the Omnipotent, and dream
The universe has wandered from its course
To thwart thy love? Others have lived and died
And suffered, and the long procession moves

Inexorably on.   When thou art dust
God's lips will scarce have sipped the eternal years   ·
Of justice.

Piera.

If the sword that murdered him
Had sought my heart as well, I would have blessed it,
And called the stroke my marriage to my love.
If but to-day had passed, and I were his,
And then the blow had fallen, I could have seen
Some mercy in it.   But to lose him now
Without a word, to dream away the hours
While he was lying cold — ah, verily
I am an exile from the love of God ;
The saints to whom I prayed are impotent !

Tora.

Hast thou forgot that 't is thy wedding-day ?
Is this a time for blasphemous despair ?

Piera.

In all the world what now is left for me ?

Tora.

For thee is light or darkness, for the path
Of sorrow leads to both.   A million saints
Have found such glory at the end of it
As passes happiness ; but for the weak —
It lures them to the pit.   Thy lord was brave,

And wilt thou be a coward? Duty was
His guiding star. Wouldst thou be true to him
If thou shouldst fail to do thy part in the world,
Listening humbly to the voice of God?

Piera.
What shall I do? I am alone — alone,
My sister.

Tora.
So — 't is good that thou shouldst weep.
Tears are God's dew for sorrow — let them fall!
Richer than pearls are they, more potent far
Than minted gold. Weep on, but when thou hast done
Let wrath possess thy soul.

Piera.
In God's name, whom
Dost thou suspect?

Tora.
If that pernicious soul
Who clamors for suspicion in my brain
Know aught of this, the tortures of the damned
Would be light punishment.

Piera.
Ah, pity me!
Who is it? In this woful labyrinth
Give me some clue.

Tora.

I will not sleep for searching.
It is not fit I speak without the proof;
The thought is but a cobweb in my mind.
Let me but find a thread slight as a hair
And it is yours.

Piera.

To whom shall I appeal
If you deny me ?
[Enter the King. Piera falls, sobbing, to her knees at his feet.]
Sire !

The King.

Nay, child — I know.
This damnéd news has stabbed me to the soul.
Poor bride ! poor lady ! Have I any power
To give you comfort ?

Piera.

Give me death or justice —
Both, if you can be merciful!

The King.

This deed
Shall be avenged — I swear it by the cross,
And by the sacred blood of all the saints.

Piera.

He was so kind !

The King.
Not ours a reign of fear —
Hate armed with murder sheathed in secrecy.
The old mad doom of Italy is ours
If order be enslaved.   Thy murdered lord
Was dearest in our love, and shall he now
Die like a rat here in our very halls,
And his assassin live ?

[Enter Florimond, unperceived.]

That wide-mouthed wound
Shall not appeal in vain.   Trust to the state,
Essay no private stroke for his revenge,
And we will know the truth, and the red hand
That struck him down shall follow to the grave :
I promise it.

Florimond.   [Advancing.]
Most righteous is the word.
Dear lady, I can long for nothing now
Except to serve thee.

Piera.   [To Tora.]
Take me back to him —
My husband !

Tora.
Then the guilty all must die,
Whoever they may be ?

The King.

Have I not sworn it ?

Tora.

Amen !   May Christ have mercy on the souls
Of all of us !

[Exeunt Tora and Piera.]

The King.

What enemies had he,
Or private quarrels that we knew not of ?

Florimond.

I never knew a creature better loved.
He had a thousand friends, but not a foe —
Or so I thought ; yet I know naught of him
These many months.

The King.

Arouse Prince Andrea,
And say we wish to speak with him.

[Exit Florimond by a side door; he is heard clamoring without.]

Florimond.

My lord !
Come forth ! the king desires you — wake, my lord !

The King.

Is it in vain that I have planned and toiled,
And struck great blows for punishment, to give

Laws to my country, and to make her strong
Under the rule of order ?   Must I now
See feuds grow fierce and know not where to strike ?
I will not suffer it.   The state shall know
And punish, that revenge may be disarmed,
And the great house whereof he was the head
Fail not in loyalty.

[Enter Florimond and Prince Andrea, by the side door.   As they
enter Florimond speaks aside to the Prince.]

Florimond.
Fear no betrayal
From me, my lord.   I have not said a word.

The Prince.
What should I fear ?

[Florimond bows himself out, but returns unobserved to a sheltered
nook at the rear, where he remains during the following
dialogue.]

The King.
Advise me, Andrea.
You know this news ?

The Prince.
Leone's death ?   I know it.

The King.
What shall we do ?   A crime so infamous
Cannot be fitly punished.   Stabbed to death

Upon his wedding-morning — one so true,
Whose house was always loyal to our rule —
Our noblest subject and our dearest friend.
The vile assassin who has robbed us of him
Shall die a thousand deaths.

The Prince.
                              Your tongue 's a fool!
I killed him — I !
                    The King.
                    You killed him !

                    The Prince.
                              It was I !
Will you not hear ?   I killed him like a dog !
Thank God that he is dead !

                    The King.
                         Why did you kill him ?

                    The Prince.
My reason was sufficient.   He deserved
The furnace or the rack.

                    The King.
                         What was your reason?

                    The Prince.
Are you not satisfied ?   I say 't was good,
And more I will not say.

The King.

By heaven, you will !
Or the black question shall extort the truth.

The Prince.

Am I afraid ? God ! this is dangerous !
My tongue is mine, to wag it as I will.
The torture will not move it.

The King.

I have sworn
Leone's murderer shall follow him
Down to the grave. I swore it by the cross,
And by the sacred blood of all the saints.
His virgin-widow's tears shall be avenged.
Give me the cause that I may fix the guilt
Where it should be, or by my oath in heaven
Your head shall suffer.

The Prince.

All the guilt is mine.
None aided, none conspired. I struck him dead
With this my sword. Do as you will with me.

The King.

Oh, this is death ! Andrea, my son, my son !
Wilt thou not tell me ? Surely it was grave,
Thy cause for such a deed. Reveal it all,

And I will warrant thee against the world,
And crave the Holy Father on my knees
To free me of my vow.

The Prince.
Fulfil it, rather.
I do not fear to die.   My youth has passed
Over a lovely country flecked with flowers.
What time more fitting for the swoop of death,
Ere yet the skies grow dull, and the bleak wastes
Stretch nightward round my soul?   Fulfil thy vow,
And I will bless thee that my day of joy
Shall have no night of sorrow.

The King.
Andrea !
Hast thou forgot our love ?   Hast thou forgot
The day thy mother died ?   She bade us live
As friends and brothers — knitted soul to soul,
Even as in marriage — and we pledged it there.
We have been one in thought, and shall this specter
Rise like a blight between us ?   Tell me all.
When have I failed thee ?   If this blow was thine
Why then 't is mine as well.   If thou hast suffered
My heart is rived an hundred-fold.   My son,
Canst thou not trust me ?
I have yielded oft
My will to thine.   When thou wast but a child

And the great house of Vancua was doomed,
I saved its youngest heir to be thy friend
Because thy heart was moved to pity him.
When thou didst name the woman of thy love
I suffered thee to wed her, though the state
And all the world opposed me; and my heart
Has claimed her as mine own.

The Prince.

He slandered her—
It was for that I killed him. When I left you
He stood beside that door and whispered me
A most abusive tale — of her, my wife,
And Florimond, my friend. Conspiracy,
Murder, and poison were its elements.
I smote him with my sword. You would have done
The same, if you had heard. I struck him down,
Walked in upon his fell conspirators,
And drank the wine he warned me of— and see—
I am not dead!

The King. [Aside.]
And thus thy day of joy
Shall have no night of sorrow. God in heaven,
Thou dost fulfil my vow.

The Prince.
I am the son
Of one who held the honor of his wife

As sacred as the chalice of our God —
Of one who would have scorched the impious hand
That dared pollute the whiteness of her robe.
If it were she whom slander had assailed,
What would my sire have done ?

The King.

He would have killed.
And thou, his son and hers, couldst do no less.

The Prince.

Thank God !

The King.

Leone's doom was in the stars —
God willed it.   On thine uncorrupted soul
His blood shall never rest !

The Prince.

May scorn and wrath
Part us no more !   Now could I die for thee —
For thy rash vow.

[The Prince is seized with a spasm, under which he sinks to a
    couch, writhing in pain and unconscious.   The King stands
    over him.]

The King.

It is the Persian poison —
Do I not know it ?   Death has clutched him now
With one red hand — perchance to play with him

And toss him back to life.   Mother of Christ!
If I have ever served thee for an hour,
Rend him one hour from death!   Oh, give him back
Ere the dark wings fold blinding over him
For all eternity!
                    The doom has fallen.
The structure I have builded is aflame,
Falling to ashes.   I can work no more.
I, who destroyed that we might build anew,
Am met by the destroyer, and my dream
Of union for discordant Italy,
Whose soul was once the empire of the world,
Lies here in ruins.   Deadly Italy!
Thou sepulcher of nations, on whose portal
Curses are writ for hope, and sneers for love,
Whose shrine is strewn with bones and dashed with
        blood
Of heroes numberless, how long, how long
Must thy sons die for thee, and die in vain!
Where is thy throne, where is thy regal crown
Among the nations?   Buried deep in shame,
Where thou liest sunken in a sullen sleep.
We call thee, and our cries thou wilt not hear —
We draw thy sword, yet cannot rouse thy soul.
Beware lest thou awake to slavery —
Lest the barbarian kings descend on thee
And bind thy fatal loveliness in chains!
        [The Prince quietly recovers consciousness, and rises.]

143

The Prince.

What is there ill with me ?

The King.

Nay, all is well

With thee, my son.

The Prince.

Such dizziness I feel —

The King.

Lean here a moment — it will pass away.
We will go talk together — thou and I.
Strange dreams of death and life came to my sleep
Last night.   We 'll talk of them, and for an hour
Forget that we are kings — insatiate
Breeders of nations, conquerors of strife.

The Prince.

Strange counsel !   Thou wouldst have me for an hour
Forget my destiny !   Is this my father ?

The King.

Come, we will go and look upon the sea —
The sea is blue to-day.

The Prince.

What was thy dream ?

[Exeunt the King and the Prince.   Florimond advances unperceived.]

Florimond.

He knows the truth, and when the prince is dead,
What death too hideous for us? Farewell,
My noble patron! When we meet again
I 'll greet thee like a Vancua, and claim
A reckoning for the past. Most noble lady,

[Calling softly at the side-door.]

Open to me, for I have news indeed.

[Valeria opens the door and appears.]

The king knows all, and thou must flee with me
From his revenge.

Valeria.

The night is over now.
I have a thing or two to say to thee,
And then may the God of mercy and of love
Grant I may never see thy face again
In this world or the next.

Florimond.

Valeria !
Speak not, but hear me ! He has told him all,
And through his wrathful innocence the king
Has read the truth. The instant of his death
Will be our doom.

Valeria.

So be it !

145

Florimond.

What say'st thou ?

Hast thou grown mad ?

Valeria.

No — no !   Once I was mad,
But one fierce moment wrapped my soul in flame
And it was purged.

Florimond.

Dost thou not understand
'T is death to linger here ?   If they should spare thee
Our retribution could not, for to-night
The infuriate mob will slip the tyrant's leash —
This hated race will perish, and these halls
Will be chastised with fire.   To-morrow morn
Thou shalt awake to happiness and power
If thou but dash these vague misgivings down
And go with me.

Valeria.

There is no happiness
This side the grave for me.   The arms of power
I can but wield awry.   Go — let me die —
'T is only in my shroud I shall be safe.

Florimond.

Sweet lady, there are many million years
Beyond this day's despair.   Full well I know

That from the tense strain of a mighty deed
The soul recoils to agonies of doubt.
Thy mind has leaped the centuries, and dared
A stroke for fate and immortality,
And now black clouds envelop thee.   Be brave —
They cannot linger long ; soon thou shalt see
Visions of glory and delight once more.
Hast thou forgot our love ?

Valeria.
Beware of me !
I have been patient long, but when thou speak'st
That word, I long to blast thee with a breath.
I never loved thee, and with all my soul
I do despise thee now.

Florimond.
How dar'st thou tell
These lies to me ?

Valeria.
A noble patriot —
Who prates of fate and immortality
And love all in a breath !   For which of these
Was murder done?   Was it for liberty,
God, and the people that we poisoned him ?
So said'st thou, and the spell was over me,
And I believed.   Or was it for revenge,
The satisfaction of our secret hate,

That we destroyed this hero — I, his wife,
And thou, his friend ?

Florimond.

Art thou so mean a thing —
A poor, weak woman after all ?   Alas !
I was a fool to trust thee, to believe
Thy soul roused to great issues.   Yesternight
I found thee starved, caged, shrunken, in despair.
I showed thee all the world, and a great cause
To live and die for, and methought I found
A man's brain wielded by a woman's zeal,
A child of liberty, who laid her head
Upon her mother's breast, and wept for joy
That she could serve her.   Canst thou in a night
Forswear thine ancestry, and fill thy veins
With tyrant's blood ?

Valeria.

God ! is it but a night
That I have lived since then ?   'T was long enough
For the wide world to age in, long enough
To learn that naught in all the universe
Is half so precious as a stainless soul.

Florimond.

Unsullied was thy soul until this hour.
To free a million by the death of one —

'T is to be pure like fire, and brave like steel.
The narrow standards of the past will bind
Free minds no more. A new philosophy
Widens the bounds of virtue, tears away
The lean monk's blinding cowl, and dares reveal
The beauty and the glory of this world
Priests have so long defamed and kings despoiled.
The sword of justice must reclaim for man
His stolen heritage. That sword was thine.
Thy deed might be the halo of a saint,
So holy was it. Italy is cursed
With many tyrants. When the last has fallen,
And she stands free beneath her glowing skies,
Such strokes will shine like jewels in the crown
Of her redemption.

Valeria.

Let me prophesy !
The mantle of the seer becomes thee not.
Not thus will Italy be saved. Her vice
Will never thus redeem her from her shame.
Though murder grow as trite as tyranny
And treachery as custom-stale as hate,
Her doom will speed the faster. It is writ
That sin brings punishment, and years of woe
Must follow years of wrath. For times like these
Long centuries of penance shall unroll
Ere Italy be worthy to be free.

Florimond.

The future is thy kingdom, prophetess.

Valeria.

Be warned then — flee! Man cannot baffle God.
Thy hope is doomed — the blight of greed is in it.
Though ruin sweep a road wide as the sea
Thou shalt not touch the goal of thy desire.

Florimond.

By all the saints! you have communed with fate
Since last I saw you.

Valeria.

　　　　　　'T is most true, indeed.
My life has known despair and misery,
And blesséd hope and moments of high joy,
And thirst, and longing, and the love of truth;
But in that instant when my husband drained
Our cup of death, it knew them all forever.
The past rose over me in rolling waves
Of mighty memories. I saw the truth,
And took her hand again, and all was clear.
And through the endless watches of this night
I sat communing with her face to face,
While he whose ill-starred love we had betrayed
Slept his last hours away. My soul is armed

Against thee now.   The spell inscrutable
That made my mind thy slave dissolves in light,
And I am free.

Florimond.

This is thy gratitude !
The love of many years, the zealous service
In spite of bitter perfidy, the long
Devotion to a dream, the dear desire
To crown one thwarted life with happiness;
A great cause risked, and death defied — all these
Are scorn to thee !

Valeria.

Speak'st thou of gratitude ?
That theme is not at home upon thy lips.
I seem to hear my husband say those words.
He gave me all — 't is late for gratitude,
Now that my thankless hand has stolen all
From him ; yet I will give it, and be true
From now until the end.

Florimond.

He has not changed.
If all were as before, if he could live
And play the king forever, he would be
Insufferable still to thy free soul
As he was yesterday.

151

Valeria.

What boots it now ?
Our hands and destiny have brushed away
That problem. If I cannot live with him,
Then I will die with him.

Florimond.

Insensate thing !
Know'st thou what thou invokest ?

Valeria.

Death.

Florimond.

Ay, death.
But not the soft embrace of perfumed peace,
A bower of poppies where the soul may sink
Into eternal rest, where holy thoughts
May fan away all stinging memories,
And lull the baffled spirit into dreams
Of infinite fulfilment — not to thee
Will death come thus, if thou demand it now.
Disgrace, a public doom and punishment,
The torture, and a lingering agony
Men pale to think of, madden to endure,
Will lead thee to the grave.

Valeria.

And through the pain
I shall behold innumerable years

Thronging the spaces of eternity,
And hear the song of rapture from afar.

Florimond.

Impalpable creation of a dream,
What wouldst thou do? Think, if the power of thought
Lives in the filmy chambers of thy brain.
Behind, disaster; and before thee, shame;
And dim oblivion beyond — a world
Unpeopled, save in wild imaginings
Of maddened zealots, unexplored and dire.
Take the bright cup of life, full to the brim,
And go with me.

Valeria.

The voices in my ear
Are sweeter far than thine. They offer me
A whole eternity of joy within
Life's little minute that is left to me.
What matters immortality? My soul
Feels the wide winds, lives in the quenchless light
For one swift hour. Eternity could do
No more. Whether this death be death indeed,
Or but the portal to a nobler life,
I am content to die.

Florimond.

These vaporings —
Thou baffling demon of perversity —
These shall not balk me. I will have thee yet —

[Tries to seize her.]

Valeria.

Thou shalt not touch me! I have done with thee
Forever!

Florimond.

Wilt thou make me mad as thou?
I love thee — dost thou hear? Thou murderous woman,
If the red blood upon thy hand were mine
Still would I love thee.

Valeria.

Wilt thou prove my words
Already?

Florimond.

Thou wast mine — my twin — my queen.
Our troth was registered in hell, and sealed
In blood. Thou canst not leave me in the lurch,
And die with fine words on thy lips.

Valeria.

And this
Is the deliverer! Speak to me no more!

[The marching of armed men is heard without.]

Florimond.

Hear'st thou that sound? Now shalt thou choose in-
deed.
'T is the king's guard, coming to lead us hence
To his tribunal. Choose — their arms or mine.

I shall escape — some of them are my friends.
Let me but clasp thee, and thou too art safe.
Life, and the world to reign in, and the love
Of one who reads the secrets of thy soul,
Of one whose heart is but an instrument
Tuned to thy finest measures.   Come to me —
The old Valeria I knew of yore.

Valeria.

I know thee not.   My soul is winged for God,
And has forgotten thee forevermore.

[Enter the King's Guards.]

Captain.

In the king's name I do arrest ye both.

Valeria.

God bless you for it !

Florimond.

Woman, thou hast been
Destructive as a pest, false as a lure.

Valeria.

There is no sin that cannot be redeemed.

[Florimond feigns a few desperate sword-thrusts, and escapes.
Valeria yields herself, and is borne away.]

[Curtain.]

ACT V

ACT V

SCENE.—Same as Act II. Enter the Captain of the Guards with nearly half the guardsmen, and a few courtiers, including Filippo.

Captain.

Great deeds are on the wing.   We must prepare.
The long night gladdens to the dawn, and now
Day's harbingers awake and sing.   My friends,
The prince is dying.

Filippo.
Thus the enemies
Of liberty must perish !

[Some make signs of joy; some receive the news with awe-stricken silence.]

Captain.
Not a man
Shall fail in duty.   Each depends on all,
And all on each.   Will you be faithful, friends ?
And is all ready for the sacred hour ?

Guardsmen.

We swear it !

Others.

Put us to the proof !

Captain.

[To Filippo, whom he gradually draws away.]

My lord,
Go to the count.   Bid him not wait an hour.
The king has sent us here to the hall of justice,
And bade us open wide the doors.   Bid him
Send in his people with the rabble.   Say
The princess lies in chains since his escape ;
The king has heard — I know not what — but 't is
Some echo of the truth.   It is not safe
To wait until to-night — to give him time
To arm, and guard, and save himself, and balk
Our dear revenge.   Now that the prince is dead
We need fear nothing.

Filippo.

Dying, but not dead.
'T was neatly done, but 't is not finished yet.

Captain.

I saw him lying breathless —

Filippo.

Yes, I know,
But 't is a tricky poison — Vancua

Ought to have used a speedier. And his ruse
Did not deceive the king, who knows too well
The scope of all the poisons.

Captain.

Yet it kills—

Filippo.

Oh, surely. But he may survive this spasm ;
The first is seldom fatal.

Captain.

'T is the second.

Filippo.

Indeed ! He is well-nigh safe then. Yet I know
My father had a cousin lived through two
And died not till the third.

Captain.

What difference ?
He cannot harm us now. Go to the count —
Tell him how all things stand, and bid him haste.
We will await his bugle.

Filippo.

I am gone.
When next we meet —

Captain.

No throne will shadow us.

[Exit Filippo. The Captain goes to the door and blows three
short blasts on his bugle.]

Go you, Bernardo, bid them ring the bell
That calls the people hither.   You, my friends,

[Addressing six of the guardsmen.]

My six stanch brothers, open with this key
The great bronze doors, and guard them. Do not fear.
Watch for my signal ; be alert and swift.
You that remain, stand by the throne with me.

[Enter the rest of the Guard, one by one.   They form.]

Take the side passage, men.   You, range yourselves
Along this wall.   Now all is done, I think,
And the king's orders are obeyed.   To arms !

[Enter, in the people's division of the hall, certain citizens.   Gradu-
    ally others come in until, by the time the King enters, a dense
    throng has assembled.]

First Citizen.

What are we summoned for ?

Second Citizen.

Some war, perhaps.
Some new town must be taken, and our trades
Must pay the price.

First Citizen.

Still growling ?   If the king
Could grasp all Italy, you 'd mumble out
That 't was not worth the handling.

162

Second Citizen.

Well — I say
Home 's good enough for me.   I 'll shake no hands
Except my friends', and share no government
With smooth-tongued southerners.

First Citizen.

Have you no eyes ?
Who reaps the profit of our greatness ?   We.
Would you have been as rich in little Locca ?
Say — tell me that ?

Second Citizen.

Would I have been as rich ?
I am the foremost blacksmith in the city.
What has the government to do with that ?

First Citizen.

You are a fool !

Second Citizen.

Nay — I am not a fool —

Third Citizen.

Have you heard the news?   The Count Leone 's mur-
    dered,
And this is for the trial.

Second Citizen.

Leone murdered?

Then we shall have no wedding pageant.

Third Citizen.

True —

But there will be a splendid funeral,

And funerals are grander.

First Citizen.

Who is guilty?

Third Citizen.

How should I know? The king will answer that.

Second Citizen.

See — let us take those places by the pillar.

Come — they 'll be taken. We can see all there.

[They pass on, and continue talking among themselves and to others as they come in.]

Fourth Citizen.

Too long have we been governed by a king —

We 'll teach him that.

Fifth Citizen.

Ay — Vancua was right.

He has spilled our blood, and drained our treasuries.

He shall die for 't.

Fourth Citizen.

This earth shall soak his blood
That he has trod as king.

Sixth Citizen.

Ay — king, forsooth!
Here where our sires were free. This upstart king,
And the great house of Vancua 'neath his heel!

Fifth Citizen.

He shall die for 't — he and his murderous son.

Seventh Citizen.

'T is strange about Leone's death. I thought
That prince too brave to play the assassin.

Sixth Citizen.

Yet
No sooner had his friend offended him
In some slight quarrel — so said Vancua —
He whips me out his sword and runs him through,
And lies down to as sweet a night of slumber
As if his prey had been an oyster.

Fifth Citizen.

'T is
A tyrant, like his sire; born to it, bred to it.
We 'll make an end to all of them.

Seventh Citizen.
Be still.
The silken gossips of their court approach.

[Enter, gravely and silently, several ladies and gentlemen of the court, all wearing mourning badges. Lastly, Liperata, Tora, and Piera, clad in black. They station themselves near the throne. During the following scene, while these converse together in the front of the stage, people of all classes gradually fill the hall.]

Third Citizen.

Look at the bride, poor thing — that was to be.
Troth ! she is pale.

Second Citizen.
But not a tear in the eye !
Faith — she should wring her hands, and weep, and
wail,
And cry for vengeance. Zounds! she is a stone.

First Citizen.

Lord ! would you measure sorrow by the gallon ?

Third Citizen.

Look ! the king's sister and his niece, in black.
Can this be for the count ?

Second Citizen.
And why not, pray ?
They loved him well.

166

First Citizen.

'T is strange.

Tora.

O mother, mother !
Dost thou remember when he came from the war
And we stood here, as now?

Liperata.

Yes, child.

Tora.

This day
Is terrible, but not so sad as that.
He is but dead — my prayers can speed his spirit.
But to be still while he gave up his soul
Unto unworthiness — ah ! that was pain !

Liperata.

He died untainted, dear. Think not he loved her.
He loved a dream and set her face within it,
Even as some heathen might enshrine in gold
A monstrous image, hallowing it with prayers.
God takes the worship that is meant for him,
Though ignorantly offered.

Tora.

Dost thou think
The earthly contact of his soul with hers
Must last forever ?

Liperata.

Is the heathen saint
Chained to his idol through eternity?
Nay, God is just.   Their souls have never touched.

Tora.

Ay, all will yet be well.   This earth shall feel
The hand of God to-day.   Look up, Piera;
God will avenge our woe.

Piera.

Think not of me.
I try no more to solve God's problems for him —
They are too hard.   I do not understand
The forces which have wrecked us.   They must come
From the black voids of space—they are so strange,
So strange and terrible.   Shall I mock with tears
The whirlwind's anger?   Shall I cry aloud
When all the thunders of a thousand years
Are echoing through the caverns of my soul?

Tora.

Ay, all the more ; till God shall hear thy voice.

Piera.

Nay, nay ; I am a watcher on the shore
Of some dead world.   There was a shock, a crash ;
The elements grew bolder than their wont,
The green earth reddened, and the stars shot fire,
And all was done.   I am too slight a thing

To move a dog to soothe my loneliness.
I ask nothing of God, save to go pray.

Liperata.

What puts thee in this strange mood, child?

Piera.

Alas!

When my love died I mourned. But now I see
Whole kingdoms are adrift ; and what am I
That I should hug a private grief, invoke
A special vengeance! Nay, if God be just,
Leave it to him!

Tora.

Yet even on earth, at times,
His sword strikes home. Is not Valeria
In chains? This day our woe shall be avenged.

Piera.

Blood — ever blood ! 'T is man's revenge, and not
God's justice.

Tora.

Dost thou hear?

[The strains of a monks' chant are heard in the distance, gradually
growing louder, and then fading away to silence.]

Holy mother, maid divine,
Thus we bear him to thy shrine —
Pray for him !

In the earth his clay shall rest ;
Lift his spirit to thy breast.
                    Pray for him !

Not through purgatorial flame
Let him supplicate thy name —
                    Pray for him !

Martyr-winged, his soul doth rise
To thy throne in paradise.
                    Pray for him !

Tora.

                    O God ! O God !

Liperata.

The prince goes to the chapel.   Be at peace.
This journey does not weary him, my child.

Piera.

Why dost thou tarry here ?   The convent walls
Will hush all deadly noise, and Christ thy Lord
Has called thee.   Wilt thou go ?

Tora.

                    When all is done.

Piera.

I will go with thee.   Not the nun's deep veil,
The funeral pall, the vows that bury life,
Shall hide my love from thine.   We will go pray —
The poor world needs it.   We will think away
The wilful years, and pray for all the world
Until we die.

Tora.

May death come soon, my sister !

Piera.

Not sooner than the light. I would not grope
Through all eternity. Nay, give God time
To teach us.

[Enter the King, in full royal robes, crowned and sceptered. As he
advances and seats himself upon the throne, a wave of murmur-
ing passes over the people.]

Fourth Citizen.

See — the king's alone !

Voices. [Softly.]

The prince !

Third Citizen.

Where is the prince ?

Second Citizen.

The pretty princess, too ?

Others.

The prince !

First Citizen.

Nay — it is strange.

Seventh Citizen.

What fools are these,

To lick the heels that crush them !

171

Fourth Citizen.

Where is he ?

But the prince!

Fifth Citizen.

Where he should be.   Trust the count.

The King.

My people !   Ye have heard me many times —
Now for the last time hear !   I have grown old
In serving you.   The crown you gave to me
I have enriched with principalities,
The scepter I have girded round with laws —
Now are they yours again.   I loved my country.
I thought to make her orderly and strong,
To gather 'neath her shield all Italy
Against the foreign foe.   But sinuous fate
Has baffled me ; the evil of the times
Unwinds its coils, and lo! God's instrument
Lies dead.   My people, I can work no more.
Prince Andrea, whom ye loved, who dipped your flag
In shining victory, who would have borne it
Far to the heights where glory sits enthroned
Above time's siege, who loved you with a love
More strong than death, who would have made you
        free
Beyond the hope of those who dare betroth
Blasphemous impotence with liberty,
Who would have made you great beyond their power —
Prince Andrea is murdered.

Many Voices. [Softly.]
   Murdered !

Others.
         Listen !
The prince is dead.

    The King.
    He gave you cities, gold,
A great hope, a great destiny : and you —
You give him death !

     Many Voices.
     Not we !

     Others.
        No, no — not we !
Show us the murderer !

    Seventh Citizen.
     What does this mean ?
Is it the count's work ?

    Fifth Citizen.
     By Saint Michael's sword ! —
He should have told us this.

    Fourth Citizen.
     He trusts us not.

    Seventh Citizen.
Nay, doubt him not. Wait — wait !

First Citizen and Others.

Who killed him!

Voices.

Oh,

Our warrior!

The King.

My people, are ye true?
And do they slander you who dare assert
You were false traitors to his love?

First Citizen.

Who dares?

Tell us who says it?

Sixth Citizen. [Aside to his faction.]

Where is Vancua?

Seventh Citizen.

'T is going strangely.

Fifth Citizen.

Faith, he sleeps!

Sixth Citizen.

Alas!

These golden sands of time are slipping fast —
What shall we do?

Voices.

Give us the villain!

First Citizen and Others.

Justice !

The assassin !

The King.

Friends, I must believe you true.

My soul shall trust you, for the power ye gave me
Is yours again, your glory or your shame
Through coming years. I love my country still,
And now that I can guide her course no more—

Voices.

No ! No !

Others.

The king !

Many Voices. [Shouting.]

The king !

Seventh Citizen. [To some of his faction.]

Ye cowards ! knaves !

What ! are you cheering him ?

Fifth Citizen.

What can we do ?

The Multitude. [Cheering.]

Long live the king !

The King.

It cannot be, my people.

My scepter now must be the pilgrim's staff,

My robe his cowl. In far Jerusalem
My prayers shall plead for you. But ere I go,
Before I dare resign my stewardship,
One duty lies before me, unto you
One service I can render. Oh, my people,
Will you have justice? Shall this noisome crime,
That darkens o'er us like a pestilence,
Rise festering to God?

                    First Citizen.
                    The murderer !

                    Many Voices.
Give us the murderer !

                    Others.
                    Tear him limb from limb !

                    The King.
Be patient — ah, you shall have need of patience.
                    [To the Guard.]
Bring in the woman, and protect her well.
                    [Exit Captain with six men.]
Be still, be patient. Let this cause be tried
All orderly, that justice may not frown
Upon our offering. Be nearer gods
Than men, my people ; for your souls must bear
A tale of treachery and ingratitude
Unmatched among the devil's miracles,
And not go mad.

Tora.

Ah, mother, she is coming.

Liperata.

Hush ! she is come.

[Re-enter the Guard with Valeria in chains.]

Many Voices. [Murmuring.]
The princess !

First Citizen.

This is false !

Second Citizen.

How do you know?

First Citizen.

She kill her husband ?   Look !

'T is false, I say.

Piera.

Ah, Tora, sister mine,
There 's more in this than we can understand.
See — is she not a seraph straight from God,
Standing with folded wings?

Tora.

It is hell's way —
To counterfeit heaven's splendor with its flame.

Piera.

Beware ! beware !   Thou know'st not heaven and hell.

The King.

Valeria, widow of Andrea, prince,
Co-ruler of this realm, and heir of all
Its principalities, stand forth, and hear.

[Valeria steps forward a pace or two, free of the Guards.]

I summon thee to answer for the death
Of Andrea, thy husband ; warranted
By his confession, made in ignorance,
But clear unto the wise.   Base-born wast thou ;
His name redeemed that stain.   Thy lot was mean ;
He raised thee to a throne.   Thou wast a beggar ;
He gave thee splendor.   A wandering outcast, thou ;
He made thy home a palace, and thy vassals
The noblest in the land.   Thou wast despised,
The sport of men, fore-doomed to be their slave ;
And he whose heart was stainless as the morn
Gave thee his love.

First Citizen.

Her soul weeps tears of blood -
What does this mean ?

The King.

And for these gracious gifts,
Thou, three months from the altar where thy vows
Were registered for God, thou didst conspire
His ruin.   Thou didst play upon his trust,
Until in thy defense, to vindicate
Thy honor, — dear to him though cheap to thee, —

He killed the friend whose truth had dared to assail it,
And drank thy poison like ambrosial wine,
Sure of its purity as though he had seen
The angels brew it for the lips of Christ.

Voices. [Softly.]
Oh, horrible! is it true?

The King.
Thou hear'st the charge.
If thou canst meet it, or if thou dost ask
Another voice to plead thy cause for thee,
Speak, and avoid thy doom.

Valeria.
I do confess
The truth of these thy charges, and I ask
The sentence of the law.

Voices.
Death!

Many Voices. [In great cries.]
Death!

[The Guards draw near to protect her.]

Tora.
Hear'st thou?

Piera.
She is calm still.   What do we know —
We mortals!

The King.

Ye have heard.   Unhappy woman,
Thou dost avow thy guilt.   For crimes like thine
The law gives death prolonged with agony,
And thou hast heard the people ratify
The law's decree.   Yea, on thy perjured soul
God shall pass sentence ; ere this day is old
Thou diest.   Yet because thou wast the wife
Of Andrea, and a princess, death shall come
With deference, as though the blood of kings
Flowed in thy veins.   Woman, prepare thy soul.
Choose thou the means of death.

Valeria.

The means of death !

Captain of the Guard.   [Aside to Valeria.]
Gain time !   The count —

Valeria.

Nay, thus then !

[She draws a small dagger from her girdle, and plunges it into her
breast.]

Oh, my soul —
How light it is !

The King.

Will such a narrow door
Suffice for death to enter ?

Valeria. [Dreamily.]

Do not fear.

Ah, sire, there is an angel at the point —
Death's herald. [To the Guard.] Do not touch me! I can
die
Untended.   Look, dear, it is almost done!

The King.

Give me the dagger.

[The Captain picks it up from the floor, and hands it to the King,
who shows it to the people.]

'T is envenomed black.
She dies within the hour.

[To the Captain.]   Bring hither now
Your other prisoner.

Captain.

Sire, he escaped us.

The King.

Escaped you, say you?   One against you all?

Captain.

He fled away.   Not all the winds could reach him.

The King.

It is a lie, and you who utter it —
You are a traitor.

[For some time faint cries and vague sounds of an approaching crowd
have been heard without.   Now they grow more distinct, and the
gathering uproar is plainly audible.]

Captain.

Traitor to a tyrant —

Lover of liberty !   Friends of Vancua,

Rise — to your work !

[He darts toward the King with uplifted sword; but Valeria, swift
as thought, throws herself in front of the King, and baffles the
attack.]

Valeria.

Save the king !

[There is great confusion through the hall. The Captain is seized
and pinioned by several courtiers. The noise and the cries without
grow louder and louder.]

Ah, sire,

Your throne is doomed.   Ten thousand foes unfurl

The flag of liberty.   Beware! beware !

Arm yourself!   Save yourself!   Oh, I forgot

Your danger in my ecstasy.   The count —

Ah, listen ! he and ruin are without —

What will you do ?

Voices.   [Shouting without.]

A Vancua ! Vancua !

Down with the tyrant !   Kill the king !

Seventh Citizen.

Awake !

For Vancua — liberty !

[Some of Florimond's faction try to force their way to the door, where
those without are struggling to enter.   The others contend
against them.]

First Citizen.

Protect the king !

Many Voices.

The king !

The King.

Listen, my people ! he is there —
Tempter and traitor ! He has fled my justice —
To yours I now commend him. Punish him —
This Count of Vancua who betrayed his friend !
Kill him who killed his master ! Spare him not,
Who did not spare this miserable woman,
But lured her on to crime. Oh, silence him,
Who dares profane the name of liberty
And shroud the state in ruin. Be avenged
For every lie upon his perjured soul.
Do this for justice, and my last farewell
Shall be a blessing.

Voices. [Shouting without.]

Vancua !

Many Voices. [Within.]

The king !

[The throng beyond the entrance surges in, driving the others back toward the throne. Florimond, armed, appears at the topmost step in the wide door-way, sword in air, with armed troops behind him, flanked by the mob. The two crowds struggle furiously together, pushing and surging with cries and blows.]

Many Voices. [From the King's crowd.]

The traitor !

Others.

Kill the traitor !

Shouts. [From the Vancua faction.]

Death to the tyrant !

Florimond.

On, on, friends ! Liberty ! The day is ours !

[The First Citizen has made his way to the door. He now suddenly
wrenches Florimond's sword from his uplifted hand, and plunges
it under his arm, above the protecting armor.]

First Citizen.

This — for the women you have ruined ! this —
For justice and the state !

Florimond.

Valeria !

Oh, hear me ! — Is this all ?

[Florimond falls dead. Valeria, lying half unconscious on the steps
of the throne, neither hears nor sees. The Count's friends tenderly
protect his body and bear it out; and his assailant slips back,
uninjured, in the mêlée. Fierce shouts arise from Florimond's
followers, as they surge forward into the hall.]

Many Voices. [From the Vancua faction.]

Revenge !

Filippo.

[From the topmost step, shouting to the throng without.]

See — see —

He is dead, our hero ! Kill this tyrant — kill !

The King.

Thank God ! Now all is over.

Many Voices. [Without and within.]

Kill the king!
Down with the king ! the king !

[The King steps down from his throne, and marches into the midst of the people. At the same time Cardinal Ortus appears at the door.]

The King.

Come — kill me, then.
Do I love life, now hate has poisoned it ?
Oh, kill me ! If you have forgot my laws,
The cities I have given you, and the glory —
Then kill me. I am old, and death shall be
Dear as a brother come to call me home.
I pray you, kill me !

[Silence and a pause.]

Oh, my countrymen,
Long have I loved you — ever your desire
Has been my goal. Will you have liberty ?
'T is yours. The throne is yours. And may your star,
Kindled in justice, glorified in power,
Pale not, till freedom's morn shall waken earth
To universal gladness. I have done.
Cardinal, though among mine enemies
Thou stand'st, to thee do I confide my people.
To thee, the anointed son of holy church,
I yield my crown for them.

[The Cardinal approaches, and receives the articles from the King's hands.]

To thee my scepter,
The symbol of the law; my robe as well.
Long may the state be clad in majesty,
And throned in strength.

[He stands forth in a pilgrim's robe of sackcloth, girded with rope.]

And from thy hands I ask
The benediction Rome cannot refuse
Unto the meanest of the sons of Christ
Who seek his sepulcher.

[He kneels to the Cardinal.]

Cardinal.
May God forgive
Thy crimes, usurping king ! May Christ's dear blood
Efface the blood of murdered countrymen
From thy stained record ! May thy pilgrimage
Gain pardon for this latest trick of all,
By which thou cheatest justice of the head
Which is her due !

The King.
Nay, do not touch him, friends —
The foolish, impotent, and blind old man.
Cardinal, these are wiser far than thou ;
They feel the deeper purpose of my labor,
Which wrath has hid from thee. The blood I shed
Was consecrated to a deathless hope,
That shall survive the ruin thou invokest

And meet fulfilment in the deeps of time,
Whither I send my fame.

Cardinal.
What impudence!
Thy fame is infamy, thy hope dishonor·

First Citizen.
Down with him!

Many Voices.
Silence him!

The King.
Nay, spare him, friends.
Wilt thou seek Vancua?   Thy life, my lord,
Lies at my mercy.   One command from me,
Thou diest.   If I fail to utter it
And crush this stinging serpent of revenge,
'T is not in deference to thee, but God,
Whose pitiless courier, death, has brought me word
The time is not yet ripe for my desire,
And bade me pause.   And now, since naught requires
The sacrifice of blood, let us protect
These myriad lives.
Go with him hence, my people —
Not so — my brothers, fellow-citizens!
Go to the Park of Peace, and there decree
Your government, and leave a sad old man
Here with his dead.

187

First Citizen.
Ah, sire !

Agnolo.
Our hearts are yours—
Lead us against them !

Cardinal.
Can I trust thee living ?

The King.
Fool ! fool !

Liperata. [Advancing toward the Cardinal.]
Come — will you not obey him, friends !
Ye, whom he served so long, will you not grant
His last request ?   Away ! for ye are free !
[To the Cardinal.]
I charge thee, by the past that we have shared,
Yield this revenge, and lead these angry hosts
To peace.

Cardinal.
What—thou?

Filippo. [Without.]
Nay, on ! Though he is dead
The cause can never die.   Will you forsake him ?
Impotent race ! incapable alike
Of slavery or freedom !

Liperata. [To the Cardinal.]
Dost thou hear ?

The King.

Go, go, friends !   Save the weary state from blood.
I thank you all.

Many Voices.
The king !

[The people cling around him, kneeling and kissing his garments.]

Liperata.   [To the Cardinal.]
Oh, be a man —
A leader !

[The door leading toward the chapel rolls open, and on its threshold
stands the Prince, pale as marble, and clad in flowing robes of
white.   The people nearest him start back in terror, and in a moment fear takes possession of the multitude.]

First Citizen.
Look — the dead !

Many Voices.   [In stifled cries.]
The dead !   Away !
Away !

The Prince.   [Raising his arms.]
Noise ! noise !   Shall I not sleep in peace ?
Away !

[The crowd, in panic terror, surges madly over the steps at the entrance, bearing away with them the Cardinal and Liperata, and
driving before them the throng outside.   Wild cries and groans
are heard.   The Prince glides forward a few paces.]

Voices.

Good God — he comes !   God save us !   It is death !
Away ! away !

189

Agnolo.

Is he not dead, sire?

The King.

Nay,

I know not. Go, do what a wise man can
For those thy fellow-countrymen — so lost
Without a leader! Leave me, all of you,
Oh, leave me with the dying!

[Agnolo kisses the King's hand, and rising, unsheathes his sword.]

Agnolo.

Come with me!

The state is ours to save! Away — away!

The King.

So rolls the world; not all man's flaming hope
Can light one morn on earth before its time.

[The crowd has gone, and the courtiers. None are left but the King,
the Prince, Tora, Piera, and Valeria, who still lies along the
steps of the throne.]

The Prince.

I dreamed I wandered to another world,
And found my love there. Father, am I dead?
Is this the king?

The King.

God keep the world, my son!

'T is ours no more.

The Prince.

How strange ! My God ! what is it
That lies here like a pall ? Tora, what is it
That wraps you thus ? Oh, God in heaven ! my wife —
Prostrate — in chains ! Valeria, my wife —
Look at me ! speak to me !

Valeria.

My husband — see —
I too can die.

The Prince.

Thou dying, and my soul
Still bound to earth ? God will not suffer it !

Tora.

Insensate ! wilt thou love this woman still,
Who murdered thee ? Wilt thou embrace her still,
Who lured thee to the grave ?

Piera.

Ah, Tora !

The King.

Child —
Pluck out thy scorpion's tongue !

The Prince.

It is a lie !
How dar'st thou utter it ? A stupid lie !
Unsay it, lest thou send thy soul to hell —
Tora, my comrade, play-mate !

191

Tora.

'T is the truth—

God knows it, and the woman lying there
Dares not deny it.

The Prince.

Silence! Oh, my love,

Think not of her. I know 't is false, my darling.
Mistrust me not.

Valeria.

'T is true! Forgive! forgive!

The Prince.

True? true? Thou wouldst have killed me?

Valeria.

Oh, forgive!

The Prince.

It seemed like falsehood. If it be the truth,
I must have failed thee somewhere, for thy heart
Was mine alone.

Valeria.

Thine! thine!

The Prince.

And we are dying

Together? I for thee, and thou for me?

Valeria.

Yes! yes!

The Prince.

Thank God ! naught have I to forgive.
God blesses us.   What ! is remorse so dread
That thou must die ?   The children of a king,
We 'll greet the king of darkness with a smile,
And wreathe his dusky wings with roses.   Come !
All — all is gone but love.   Come, let us dream
That 't is our wedding-day, for so it is —
To-day we shall be one in heaven.   Rise ! rise !
And give me that embrace which shall endure
Through all eternity !

Valeria.

My lord ! my king !

[She droops in his arms, and he kneels with his burden.]

The Prince.

Hush — hush, dear ! Thus I held thee first, my darling —
That day thy voice went ringing through my soul,
That day I almost lost thee.   Wait for me !
Nay — wilt thou hasten ?

[Valeria dies.]

Hush !   I hear thy song.
I cannot see thee, darling, for the light.
Ah, take me ! take me !

[The Prince rises to his full stature, and then falls dead.   The King
bows over him.]

The King.

God's heaven will be the purer,

Now thou art there.

Tora.

See — he has gone with her ;
And I am left alone.

[The convent bell rings far away.]

Piera.

Hear'st thou thy Lord ?
Come, let him teach thee.   Thou hast much to learn.

The King.

Dead ! dead ! both dead !   Great God ! thy world is
   dead !

[*Curtain.*]

POEMS—I

NIAGARA'S SONG

I

BEHOLD, they are thine, my Ontario, thine! these waters
    I give to thee.
I pour the blue lakes in thy cup like wine—a foaming
    and sparkling sea.
        And I chant thee a song
        That shall never change ;
        Thou shalt hear it as long
        As the sweet stars range
Past the purple throne of the stately night, that in silence
    doth list to me.

II

'T is my love, 't is the voice of my wooing, Ontario,
    sister and friend.
Wilt thou give me thy soul for my suing, through
    years that shall have no end ?
        I have cloven a way
        Through the rocks to thee ;

And I bid thee stay
From the clamoring sea
And repose in the lap of the glad green earth, lest thou
follow the sad moon's trend.

III

There is murmur of far-away winds in my song, there
is babbling of brooks and rills,
And the whisper of forests that darkly throng at the
crest of the purple hills;
And the lulling of leaves
For the day unborn —
Ere the swift light weaves
The gold mantle of morn,
Softly wrapping in glory some deep still pool, till its
bosom with rapture thrills.

IV

Dost thou feel the soft hush o'er the prairie, where
rivers so gently flow
That the flowers, swayed by winds unwary, peer down
at their souls below?
Ah, they whisper of love,
And the words they vow
Save the heavens above
Only I and thou
Shall hear through the thronging thunders for aye,
while the centuries come and go.

V

I bear thee the white gull's quavering cry from Supe-
rior's sculptured isles,
And the whirring of wings as the geese mount high to
form in their cloud-like files.
  In my heart is the note
   Of the glad bird's hymn,
  Who, in cooling his throat
   At a deep pool's rim,
Gave his soul to remembering waters that bore me his
pæan a thousand miles.

VI

When the sea-souled lakes lie sleeping as still as a
planet's flight,
Lie dreaming of heaven, and keeping a tryst with the
stars all night,
  When their waves roll as blue
   As the sky they adore,
  When they mirror the hue
   Of the spring ashore —
They are mine, they are thine, O my queen and my
love, with their opaline robes of light.

VII

They gather in ranks white-crested with foam, and toss
me their plumes in mirth,
As the numberless legions come marching home with a
shout that doth shake the earth ;

And the colors unfurl
Of their rainbow flag,
Till its clear stripes curl
O'er my mist-veiled crag —
Till it floats its soft web o'er the fathomless pool where
the river of storms has birth.

VIII

They bring me the summer's glory, soft crowned with
a mist of gold,
And wrap me in raiment hoary when the icy year
grows old.
And they shudder and roar
When the gray winds dash
O'er their quivering floor
'Neath the lightning's lash,
And the pale clouds flee at the call of the squall to
pavilions of gloom and cold.

IX

But I gather them close in their tumult of fright, and
I laugh as the wild winds flee;
For what storm is so proud of its perishing might as
to measure its strength with me?
It can rave but an hour
Ere I scourge it home
Where the whirlwinds cower
In my caves of foam ;
And the roar of the thunder is mine for aye, till the
hush of eternity.

X

For I come from unreckoned ages, from millions of
    years long dead,
When unwrit were the world's wide pages by life's
    unfaltering tread.
        And I sang my song
        At the dawn of time,
        As the earth grew strong
        For her fate sublime,
As she bore multitudinous creatures, and lulled them
    to sleep when their strength was sped.

When imperial man on her bosom grew to his king-
    dom of joy and pain,
I looked in his luminous eyes and knew her long
    labor was not in vain.
        For the dumb tribes bowed
        To the dauntless one,
        And he sang aloud
        To the shining sun.
By the might of his wisdom he conquered all, but me
    he can never restrain.

XII

For the past's unrecorded emotion the future must
    never lose,
For the mountains must speak to the ocean, and I
    am the voice they choose.

The doom of the old
And the hope of the new —
The winter's cold
And the summer's blue —
From time to eternity plunge and roar, while the stars
shine on and muse.

XIII

I chant thee a psalm and a threnody, my love with
the breast serene.
The praises of life and of death shall be a sweet song
in thy heart, my queen.
And forever and aye —
Till the world is still
And the light fades away
And the sun grows chill —
I shall gather the thunders and rush to thee, and in
peace on thy bosom lean.

ORIGIN OF THE TIDES.

THE moon, a lady robed in white,
  Rose o'er the bosom of the sea
And whispered : Take me! by thy might
  Embrace me, seize me, set me free
From endless bondage to the night!

The brave sea rose to do her will,
  And tossed his pale arms high in air.
The deeps responded with a thrill
  That shook far coasts and islands fair.
Yet the pale maid rode higher still.

The bold surge, wrestling with defeat,
  Threw foamy kisses high — in vain.
At last he sighed : Ah, lady sweet,
  Thou art too great! But thou shalt reign
My queen. My heart shall rise to greet
The daily dancing of thy feet.

SONG OF THE AIR.

Hush — hush ! Ah, whisper low !
  Dost thou not know
    Asleep earth lies ?
Nay — wake her not ! She hears
  The circling spheres
    Sing in their skies.

I love her. All the day
  I ward away
    The sun's fierce scorn.
All night I sob and sing,
  And cool winds bring
    To soothe the morn.

I wrap her round with blue
  Her lord looks through
    With face of fire —
With blue so soft and pure
  She can endure
    His passion dire.

And when her spirit sighs
  White clouds arise
    To soothe the glare.
When she is sad, soft rains
  Efface her stains
    And leave her fair.

And though her beauty fall
  Beneath a pall
    As gray as death,
Though by fierce tempests torn
  She lies forlorn,
    Weary of breath —

I come with footfall soft
  And lift aloft
    Her robes of woe ;
And from her lover down
  I bear a crown —
    The shining bow.

Then doth she ope her eyes
  In glad surprise,
    And smile to see
The sun's winged troops awake
  For her sweet sake,
    Her slaves to be.

And I, I lie as still
    As nights that thrill
        With dawns unborn ;
I waft away her tears
    And soothe her fears —
        Sweet wraith forlorn.

So hush !   She floats to-night
    On star streams bright ;
        Her woes are gone.
The sweet moon sings to her.
    No leaf shall stir
        Until the dawn.

IN THE BEGINNING.

When sunshine met the wave
Then Love was born,
Then Beauty rose to save
A world forlorn.

For light a thousand wings
Of joy unfurled,
And bound with golden rings
The icy world.

And color flamed the earth
With glad desire,
Till life sprang to the birth,
Fire answering fire.

And so the world awoke,
And all was done,
When first the ocean spoke
Unto the sun.

A WRECK.

Brown and old, brown and old,
　Thou liest, thy cureless wounds agape.
Blue and cold, blue and cold,
　The waves thy bare bones can not 'scape.
They were thy slaves once; to atone
They mocked thee, and thou art their own.

A RONDEAU.

When roses bloom — ah, wake, sweet May!
The still world hears a roundelay
    Athrill within the throat of spring.
    Awake! your brightest trophies bring
And speed the winter's frown away.

For glory reigns the livelong day,
And Lethean perfumes softly stray
    'Mid shining bowers where dear hopes cling
        When roses bloom.

Ah, life, not thine deep mists of gray,
Not thine black voids without a ray —
    The wide dawns flash, the young winds sing,
    My heart's bells clamorously ring,
The years throng smiling crowned with bay —
        When roses bloom.

II

CANTATA.

Sung at the dedication of the Chicago Auditorium,
December 9, 1889.

HAIL to thee, fair Chicago! On thy brow
America, thy mother, lays a crown.
Bravest among her daughters brave art thou,
Most strong of all her heirs of high renown.
Thine elder sisters from the peopled East,
Throned by the surging sea,
Lift foaming cups to pledge thy crownal feast,
Calling, All hail! to thee.
Down in the mellow regions where time dozes,
Rocked by soft winds, warmed by the lazy sun,
Sweet southern cities gather wealth of roses
To wreathe for thee the garlands thou hast won.
And the young West rings out a glad acclaim;
Children new-born to fame,
Bold sister cities, generous and free,
Call hail to thee!

From misty rivers, from the lofty plains
   Rimmed round with hoary guardians grim and old,
From the rich realm beyond, where summer reigns,
   And the warm ocean sleeps in robes of gold,
From far and near the choral praises ring —
The wise world wakes, thy festal song to sing.

The ages trailed enwrapt in dreams
   Along the tideless sea.
The marsh-grass waved in sluggish streams,
   The snipe piped bold and free.
The prairies lay beflowered and gay,
   And time knew naught of thee.

And feather-crested chieftains met
   Upon thy sandy shore,
Before their lurid sun had set
   Afar, to rise no more.
They could not hear Fate's liegemen near,
   Nor see the flag they bore.
      ı

But the soul of the river lay pondering there
   Of the wonderful days to be :
My bosom the wealth of the world shall bear
   When the white ships rest with me,
When the spirit of steam and the spirit of air
Shall waft me a race like the sunlight fair,

As strong as hope
Fate's doors to ope
To realms that are rich for the souls that dare.

And the sweet blue lake that doth dream of the sky,
Or sing of the sea when the surge rolls high,
Came crested with foam to the shell-strewn strand,
And murmured: I hear thee, O River!
My waters shall waft to land
A race for whom God the Giver
Hath opened his opulent hand.
And a fabric of purple and gold and blue,
From the rays of the morning spun,
For the robes of his joy in this kingdom new
We have woven — I and the sun.

And weary nations heard
As they dreamed on the breast of time,
Till the yearning world was stirred
With the thrill of a birth sublime.
And the spirits that wait with God —
Freedom and Faith and Power —
Looked down in men's eyes and trod
The earth, as in earth's first hour.
And they wrought for the world and sang
Till the morn with music rang:

A mighty nation shall arise,
   Whose power shall perish never ;
A valiant people, free and wise,
   The chains of hate shall sever.
      A city brave and fair
      Their flag of hope shall bear.
      In liberty and love,
      Like hosts of God above,
   Glad states shall march forever.

A rush of leathern wings
   From shadowed depths of shame
Rose thunderous ; and evil things,
   Whose brows were wheeled with flame,
      Came hissing : Nay — beware !
      Ye speed on to despair.

And one said : I am War !
   I will cleave your land in twain,
And the star-strewn blue of that banner new
   Shall be wet with a crimson rain.

Fierce Fire hissed : Would you rear
   A city of delight ?
Lo ! I will wander near
   And waste it in a night !

And Anarchy upreared
A visage haggard, bleared,
That screeched : Your flag is a brilliant rag !
Will it shine so fair
When its stripes I tear,
And its stars in the mire I drag?

And Greed sneered : Fold on fold
I will dim its hues with gold.
The light of hope shall shine no more
Beyond the night, above the roar
That darkens, maddens all the world,
When bound with gold that flag lies furled.

And all hell's brood shrieked : No !
Love dies, but hate shall grow.

But God's bright host said : Peace !
And snows of silence fell.
Fear not ! these woes shall cease —
He doeth all things well.
The morning light shall purge away each stain
That flag must bear.
Like April, smiling after every rain
More pure and fair,
The land shall wake to rapture from her pain,
Of love aware.

And when the banner city wounded falls,
    When ashes fill her halls,
Her heart shall fail not, for the suppliant years
    Shall bid her dry her tears
And come to them. New glory in her eyes,
New courage in her soul, she shall arise.

City of freedom ! city of our love!
    The golden harvests of the world are thine.
Green fields around thee, fields of blue above,
    Glad in exultant youth, in power divine,
Thou smilest on the marge of shining seas,
        Pure as their robes of light.
Strange glories trail across with every breeze —
        Slow pomp of day and night.
Enthroned in majesty, thou claimest now
    Thine heritage of beauty — robes impearled,
Mantles of purple, jewels for thy brow,
    Splendors new-wrought to rouse the aging world.
Thine they shall be. Here to thy hall of state —
    The temple of our sacred liberty,
Where young Democracy, proud priest of fate,
    Shall shout afar full many a brave decree —
Hither comes trooping a resplendent train
        Bedecked with flowers ;
The loving arts shall ease thy breast of pain
        Long golden hours.

New thoughts are thine ; new visions rise
  Before thy clear prophetic eyes.
On to the future, where the light
  Streams over fields of glory,
Thy soul doth take its morning flight
  From slumberous ages hoary.
Out of the dark an eagle to the sun
Speeds on. Awake ! 'T is day ! The night is done.

COMMEMORATION ODE.

Read and sung at the dedicatory ceremonies of the World's Columbian Exposition, on the four-hundredth anniversary of the discovery of America.

COLUMBIA ! on thy brow are dewy flowers
Plucked from wide prairies and from mighty hills.
Lo ! toward this day have led the steadfast hours.
   Now to thy hope the world its beaker fills.
The old earth hears a song of blessed themes,
And lifts her head from a deep couch of dreams.
Her queenly nations, elder-born of time,
      Troop from high thrones to hear,
Clasp thy strong hands, tread with thee paths sublime,
      Lovingly bend the ear.
Spain, in the broidered robes of chivalry,
      Comes with slow foot and inward-brooding eyes.
      Bow to her banner ! 't was the first to rise
         Out of the dark for thee.

And England, royal mother, whose right hand
  Molds nations, whose white feet the ocean tread,
Lays down her sword on thy beloved strand
      To bless thy wreathèd head ;
Hearing in thine her voice, bidding thy soul
Fulfil her dream, the foremost at the goal.
And France, who once thy fainting form upbore,
Brings beauty now where strength she brought of yore ; —
      France, the swift-footed, who with thee
      Gazed in the eyes of liberty,
        And loved the dark no more.

        Around the peopled world
        Bright banners are unfurled.
The long procession winds from shore to shore.
        The Norseman sails
        Through icy gales
To the green Vineland of his long-ago.
Russia rides down from realms of sun and snow.
        Germany casts afar
        Her iron robes of war,
And strikes her harp with thy triumphal song.
  Italy opens wide her epic scroll,
In bright hues blazoned, with great deeds writ long,
  And bids thee win the kingdom of the soul.
And the calm Orient, wise with many days,
    From hoary Palestine to sweet Japan
      Salutes thy conquering youth ;

Bidding thee hush while all the nations praise,
Know, though the world endure but for a span,
Deathless is truth.
Lo! unto these the ever-living past
Ushers a mighty pageant, bids arise
Dead centuries, freighted with visions vast,
Blowing dim mists into the future's eyes.
Their song is all of thee,
Daughter of mystery.

Alone! alone!
Behind wide walls of sea!
And never a ship has flown
A prisoned world to free.
Fair is the sunny day
On mountain and lake and stream,
Yet wild men starve and slay,
And the young earth lies adream.
Long have the dumb years passed with vacant eyes,
Bearing rich gifts for nations throned afar,
Guarding thy soul inviolate as a star,
Leaving thee safe with God till man grow wise.
At last one patient heart is born
Fearless of ignorance and scorn.
His strong youth wasteth at thy sealèd gate —
Kings will not open to the untrod path.
His hope grows sere while all the angels wait,
The prophet bows under the dull world's wrath,

Until a woman fair
As morning lilies are
Brings him a jeweled key —
And lo! a world is free.
Wide swings the portal never touched before,
Strange luring winds blow from an unseen shore.
Toward dreams that cannot fail
He bids the three ships sail,
While man's new song of hope rings out against the
gale.

Over the wide unknown,
　Far to the shores of Ind,
On through the dark alone,
　Like a feather blown by the wind;
Into the west away,
　Sped by the breath of God,
Seeking the clearer day
　Where only his feet have trod:
From the past to the future we sail;
　We slip from the leash of kings.
Hail, spirit of freedom — hail!
　Unfurl thine impalpable wings!
Receive us, protect us, and bless
　Thy knights who brave all for thee.
Though death be thy soft caress,
　By that touch shall our souls be free.

Onward and ever on,
Till the voice of despair is stilled,
Till the haven of peace is won,
And the purpose of God fulfilled !

O strange, divine surprise !
Out of the dark man strives to rise,
And struggles inch by inch with toil and tears ;
Till, lo ! God stoops from his supernal spheres,
And bares the glory of his face.
Then darkness flees afar,
This earth becomes a star—
Man leaps up to the lofty place.
We ask a little—all is given.
We seek a lamp — God grants us heaven.
So these who dared to pass beyond the pale,
For an idea tempting the shrouded seas,
Sought but Cathay. God bade their faith prevail
To find a world—blessed his purposes !
The hero knew not what a virgin soul
Laughed through glad eyes when at her feet he laid
The gaudy trappings of man's masquerade.
She who had dwelt in forests, heard the roll
Of lakes down-thundering to the sea,
Beheld from gleaming mountain heights
Two oceans playing with the lights

Of eve and morn — ah ! what would she
With all the out-worn pageantry
Of purple robes and heavy mace and crown?
　　Smiling she casts them down,
　　Unfit her young austerity
Of hair unbound and strong limbs bare and brown.

　　Yet they who dare arise
　　And meet her stainless eyes
Forget old loves, though crownèd queens these be.
　　And whither her winged feet fare
　　They follow though death be there —
So sweet, so fleet, so goddess-pure is she.
Her voice is like deep rivers, that do flow
　　Through forests bending low.
Her step is softest moonlight, that doth force
　　The ocean to its course.
Gentle her smile, for something in man's face,
　　World-worn, time-weary, furrowed deep with tears,
Thrills her chaste heart with a more tender grace.
Softly she smoothes the wrinkles from his brow,
　　Wrought by the baleful years,
Smiles sunshine on the hoar head, whispers low
New charges from the awakened will of truth —
Words all of fire, that thrill his soul with youth.
Not with his brother is man's battle here.
　　The challenge of the earth, that Adam heard,
His love austere breathes in his eager ear.

And lo! the knight who warred at love's command,
  And scarred the face of Europe, sheathes his sword,
  Hearing from untaught lips a nobler word,
Taking new weapons from an unstained hand.
With axe and oar, with mallet and with spade,
She bids the hero conquer, unafraid
Though cloud-veiled Titans be his lordly foes—
Spirits of earth and air, whose wars brook no repose.

  For from far-away mountain and plain,
    From the shores of the sunset sea,
  The unwearying rulers complain, complain,
  And throng from the wastes to defend their reign,
    Their threatened majesty.
  The low prairies that lie abloom
    Sigh out to the summer air:
  Shall our dark soil be the tomb
    Of the flowers that rise so fair?
  Shall we yield to man's disdain,
  And nourish his golden grain?
  We will freeze and burn and snare.
  Ah! bid him beware! beware!
  And the forests, heavy and dark and deep
    With the shadows of shrouded years,
  In a murmurous voice, out of age-long sleep,
    Ask the winds: What creature rude
    Would storm our solitude?
    Hath his soul no fears, no tears?

The prone rivers lift up their snow-crowned heads,
Arise in wrath from their rock-hewn beds,
  And roar: We will ravage and drown
  Ere we float his white ships down.
    And the lakes, from a mist
    Of amethyst,
Call the storm-clouds down, and grow ashen and brown.
  And all the four winds wail:
  Our gales shall make him quail.
  By blinding snow, by burning sun
  His strength shall be undone.
Then men in league with these —
Brothers of wind and waste —
Hew barbs of flint, and darkly haste
  From sheltering tents and trees;
  And mutter: Away! away!
  Ye children of white-browed day!
Who dares profane our wild gods' reign
  We torture and trap and slay.

Child of the light, the shadows fall in vain.
  Herald of God, in vain the powers conspire.
  Armed with truth's holy cross, faith's sacred fire,
Though often vanquished, he shall rise again,
Nor rest till the wild lords of earth and air
Bow to his will, his burdens glad to bear.
The angels leave him not through the long strife,
But sing large annals of their own wide life,

Luring him on to freedom.   On that field,
From giants won, shall man be slave to man?
Lo! clan on clan,
The embattled nations gather to be one,
Clasp hands as brothers 'neath Columbia's shield,
Upraise her banner to the shining sun.
Along her blessed shore
One heart, one song, one dream —
Man shall be free forevermore,
And love shall be supreme.

When dreaming kings, at odds with swift-paced time,
Would strike that banner down,
A nobler knight than ever writ or rhyme
With fame's bright wreath did crown
Through armed hosts bore it till it floated high
Beyond the clouds, a light that cannot die!
Ah, hero of our younger race!
Great builder of a temple new!
Ruler, who sought no lordly place!
Warrior, who sheathed the sword he drew!
Lover of men, who saw afar
A world unmarred by want or war,
Who knew the path, and yet forbore
To tread, till all men should implore;
Who saw the light, and led the way
Where the gray world might greet the day;

Father and leader, prophet sure,
Whose will in vast works shall endure,
How shall we praise him on this day of days,
Great son of fame who has no need of praise?

How shall we praise him? Open wide the doors
　Of the fair temple whose broad base he laid.
　Through its white halls a shadowy cavalcade
Of heroes moves o'er unresounding floors —
Men whose brawned arms upraised these columns high,
And reared the towers that vanish in the sky —
The strong who, having wrought, can never die.

And lo! leading a blessed host comes one
　Who held a warring nation in his heart;
　Who knew love's agony, but had no part
In love's delight; whose mighty task was done
Through blood and tears that we might walk in joy,
And this day's rapture own no sad alloy.
Around him heirs of bliss, whose bright brows wear
Palm-leaves amid their laurels ever fair.
　.Gaily they come, as though the drum
Beat out the call their glad hearts knew so well.
　Brothers once more, dear as of yore,
Who in a noble conflict nobly fell,
Their blood washed pure yon banner in the sky,

And quenched the brands laid 'neath these arches high —
The brave who, having fought, can never die.

Then surging through the vastness rise once more
The aureoled heirs of light, who onward bore
Through darksome times and trackless realms of ruth
The flag of beauty and the torch of truth.
They tore the mask from the foul face of wrong;
    Even to God's mysteries they dared aspire;
    High in the choir they lit yon altar-fire,
And filled these aisles with color and with song:
The ever-young, the unfallen, wreathing for time
    Fresh garlands of the seeming-vanished years;
Faces long luminous, remote, sublime,
    And shining brows still dewy with our tears.
Back with the old glad smile comes one we knew —
    We bade him rear our house of joy to-day.
    But beauty opened wide her starry way,
And he passed on.   Bright champions of the true,
Soldiers of peace, seers, singers ever blest —
From the wide ether of a loftier quest
Their winged souls throng our rites to glorify —
The wise who, having known, can never die.

Strange splendors stream the vaulted aisles along—
    To these we loved celestial rapture clings.
    And music, borne on rhythm of rising wings,
Floats from the living dead, whose breath is song.

Columbia, my country, dost thou hear?
Ah! dost thou hear the songs unheard of time?
Hark! for their passion trembles at thine ear.
Hush! for thy soul must heed their call sublime.
Across wide seas, unswept by earthly sails,
Those strange sounds draw thee on, for thou shalt be
Leader of nations through the autumnal gales
That wait to mock the strong and wreck the free.
Dearer, more radiant than of yore,
Against the dark I see thee rise;
Thy young smile spurns the guarded shore
And braves the shadowed ominous skies.
And still that conquering smile who see
Pledge love, life, service all to thee.
The years have brought thee robes most fair —
The rich processional years —
And filleted thy shining hair,
And zoned thy waist with jewels rare,
And whispered in thine ears
Strange secrets of God's wondrous ways,
Long hid from human awe and praise.

For lo! the living God doth bare his arm.
No more he makes his house of clouds and gloom.
Lightly the shuttles move within his loom;
Unveiled his thunder leaps to meet the storm.
From God's right hand man takes the powers that sway
A universe of stars.

He bows them down ; he bids them go or stay ;
He tames them for his wars.
He scans the burning paces of the sun,
And names the invisible orbs whose courses run
Through the dim deeps of space.
He sees in dew upon a rose impearled
The swarming legions of a monad world
Begin life's upward race.
Voices of hope he hears
Long dumb to his despair,
And dreams of golden years
Meet for a world so fair.
For now Democracy doth wake and rise
From the sweet sloth of youth.
By storms made strong, by many dreams made wise,
He clasps the hand of truth.
Through the armed nations lies his path of peace,
The open book of knowledge in his hand.
Food to the starving, to the oppressed release,
And love to all he bears from land to land.
Before his march the barriers fall,
The laws grow gentle at his call.
His glowing breath blows far away
The fogs that veil the coming day —
That wondrous day
When earth shall sing as through the blue she rolls
Laden with joy for all her thronging souls.
Then shall want's call to sin resound no more

Across her teeming fields. And pain shall sleep,
Soothed by brave science with her magic lore,
   And war no more shall bid the nations weep.
Then the worn chains shall slip from man's desire,
      And ever higher and higher
      His swift foot shall aspire ;
      Still deeper and more deep
      His soul its watch shall keep,
Till love shall make the world a holy place,
Where knowledge dares unveil God's very face.

Not yet the angels hear life's last clear song.
Music unutterably pure and strong
From earth shall rise to haunt the peopled skies
      When the long march of time,
Patient in birth and death, in growth and blight,
Shall lead man up through happy realms of light
      Unto his goal sublime.

      Columbia !   Men beheld thee rise
      A goddess from the misty sea.
   Lady of joy, sent from the skies,
      The nations worshiped thee.
   Thy brows were flushed with dawn's first light;
   By foamy waves with stars bedight
      Thy blue robe floated free.

Now let the sun ride high o'erhead,
  Driving the day from shore to shore.
His burning tread we do not dread,
  For thou art evermore
Lady of love whose smile shall bless,
Whom brave deeds win to tenderness,
  Whose tears the lost restore.   .

Lady of hope thou art.   We wait
  With courage thy serene command.
Through unknown seas, toward undreamed fate,
  We ask thy guiding hand.
On ! though sails quiver in the gale !—
Thou at the helm, we cannot fail.
  On to God's time-veiled strand!

Lady of beauty ! thou shalt win
  Glory and power and length of days.
The sun and moon shall be thy kin,
  The stars shall sing thy praise.
All hail ! we bring thee vows most sweet
To strew before thy wingèd feet.
  Now onward be thy ways !

III

OUR LADY OF ART.

Wʜᴏ art thou, woman wondrous fair,
  Whose face is wan with woe?
Torn are thy feet, thy brow is bare —
  Ah, whither wilt thou go?
What wailing child thy cloak doth share,
  Though icy tempests blow?

  Said she : A traveler I, who found
  This child upon the sodden ground.
  Whither God leads us we are bound.

Ah, lady, Death awakes to-night —
  I see his eyes of flame.
Come in — my hearth-fire shineth bright —
  Come bless Christ's holy name !
Thy seat shall be a throne of light,
  A silver flute thy fame.

  God keep thy house in peace, she said ;
  And guard thy soul from woful dread !
  Far lies the path my feet must tread.

'T is love implores thee.   Not in vain
  Love kneels before thy feet.
Ah, break those bitter bonds of pain
  And wear love's garland sweet.
Bright gems, rich robes without a stain
  For such a bride were meet.

*Ah! love is dear, but God hath lit
His lamp of truth. Though poor my wit,
I cannot choose but follow it.*

Nay, thou dost dream — no light is there,
  But darkness void and lone.
Deep chasms yawn thy soul to snare
  Where death shall claim his own.
The babe shrinks trembling. Ah, beware!
  Dost thou not hear his moan?

*God bade me bear the child afar.
Though we be led where tempests are,
Deep in the sky shines many a star.*

Nay, then alas! — speed on thy way,
  Hard is thy heart and proud.
Haste on! the child with us shall stay;
  Not his thy fated shroud.
He shall be strong and blithe and gay,
  His soul shall sing aloud.

He lay all naked by the path.
Ye passed him by.   God's pity hath
Made strong mine arms.   Beware His wrath!

Base-born the child! and thou art base,
  Thou strangely stubborn thing!
On to the night, and leave no trace
  Of this thy wandering.
Away! that we forget thy face —
  The madness thou wouldst bring.

Hush, hush! they cannot take thee, dear.
Thine am I still — thou shalt not fear.
These know not; now they cannot bear.

The starving winds in veils of sleet
  Wailed like thin ghosts in pain,
And eager tempests fierce and fleet
  Roared madly in their train.
But Danger at my lady's feet
  Spread all his snares in vain.

Ah, child, rest close upon my heart;
No power shall rend us twain apart,
God's hostage to my soul thou art.

And blithe and sweet, and fair and free,
  Through all the deadly place,

She bore her burden joyously,
And sped her eager pace,
And when the morn awoke in glee
A rapture filled her face.

Seest thou the light, my child? Behold—
Truth comes to earth in robes of gold,
Even as our blessed faith foretold.

And lo ! a choral song of praise
Rose from the meadows green,
And all the world was wreathing bays
To crown my lady queen;
While seraphs trooped from heaven to gaze
In golden throngs serene.

Rejoice, my child! God led us right.
Along the path we trod by night
The world comes singing in delight.

The child that lay upon her breast
Shone with a splendor rare.
Angels and men his glory blessed,
Their song became a prayer.
The choiring hosts their Lord confessed,
And knelt in worship there.

Now God be praised! awake, mine eyes,
Unworthy this divine surprise !
Here in mine arms the Christ-child lies.

240

FROM THE DARK.*

God sat enthroned in glory, with saints and seraphim
In triple rows around him, as far as heaven's rim.
And songs that rule the planets arose in waves to him.

He spake : Behold my servant, whom men and angels
    praise !
Whose hand so strong to please me, before my throne
    to raise
Temples and towers whose beauty shall gild the golden
    days ?

* " He was one of us, yet he was not. We seem all in a common crowd and all alike, or differing but in measurable degree; then we are tried by adversity, and one remains steadfast; we are tried by war, and one rises to command our commanders; and in the end we are tried by time, and one who sat with us is immortal. Others were heard in their day, but when their voices are silent his still speaks on, and is forever listened to in the assemblies of the wise. . . .

" John Wellborn Root is dead ; and this city of triumphs and misfortunes, which had high triumph in his work, has suffered in his death profoundest misfortune. The city will still be great, powerful, prodigious; but the hands — the two hands which could mold its ambition into beauty, its greatness into grandeur — are done with work. . . .

" What time·does not destroy it cherishes, what it does not wear away it makes greater; and the names of men great in art, cherished and made vast by time, weigh upon the senses of the present. Yet one

And God said : Go, mine angels, and to my servant
bear

The joy wherewith I love him, and all gifts pure and
rare.

Bid him scale heaven to know me ; even this his soul
shall dare.

Then like white words of mercy down to the aching
world

The angels bore God's message. With heaven-bright
pinions furled

They stood before his servant, and bowed their brows
impearled.

And one who shone with wisdom more splendid than
the sun

Said : Lo, I bring thee treasures from truth's high
kingdom won ;

And touch thy lips with sweetness, that God's will
may be done.

may look over the earth and say that no architect of immortal name
in any age did more for his own fame, or for the world of beauty, than
he who twenty years ago was a boy and who now is dead.

> " ' Till wasteful war shall statues overturn,
> And broils root out the work of masonry,'

he will be remembered. As long as one stone remains above another,
those stones will have a tongue to proclaim his genius. For whatever
remains will be right, just, and beautiful beyond rules. The ruins
will furnish examples for newer days."

And one whose face was lovely as dawn in summer skies
Sang softly : I am Beauty, the jewel of God's eyes ;
I bring the arts to serve thee, bright flowers of paradise.

And one whose eyes were deeper than silent seas at
 night
Said : Lo, from Christ's own heart's-blood I shaped
 this ruby bright ;
For I am Love ; I bring thee the splendor of love's
 light.

And one wove for his glory a laurel-wreath eterne —
Upon her brow prophetic a shining star did burn.
She said : The reverent ages shall list to thee and
 learn.

Then rose a gentle angel, whose eyes were veiled in
 mist,
Whose dusky wings were silvered with softest amethyst,
And all the seraphs, kneeling, his trailing garments
 kissed.

Nay, hush ! Desires ye give him ; from these I bring
 release.
Hath he not won earth's battles ? And shall the triumph
 cease ?
The war of life is over.   I bear God's crown of peace.

Ah, Lord ! Upon thy ramparts are crystal towers whose
  stones
Are suns that burn forever. Thy heaven's azure zones
Are ringed with radiant mansions, studded with shining
  thrones.

Heaven doth not need the glory earth dearly cherisheth.
Why didst thou thrill his spirit with thy celestial breath?
Bid all thine angels serve him, and give the crown to
  Death?

SHADOWS.

WHAT is most near?
Ah, sweet dead year —
Thy fallen leaf
And gathered sheaf,
The presence that is fled,
The vows that once were said —
These are most near.

Swift speeds away
Rose-crowned To-day.
So far, so far
Her light feet are !
I look and see thy face
Haunting the upland place,
Dear Yesterday.

The blooming flowers,
The sunny hours —
These cannot rest,
These are half blest.
But thou forevermore
Art mine, love, as of yore,
And time is ours.

THE LAND OF LOVE.

I saw a spirit wandering in a blessed garden land,
And, lo! she plucked seven roses and bore them in her
hand,
And wove an odorous wreath thereof, washed pure with
morning dew,
And crownéd there her shining hair for God and men
to view.

One rose was white as maidenhood, folding its heart
of gold,
And one flushed with the rapture of many a bliss un-
told,
And one grew shy and paled with dread of heavy-
footed woe.
Ah me! the fears, deep-fraught with tears, that tender blossoms know.

The fourth rose strong and stately was, and, lo! beside it stood
A tiny bud of promise, as sweet as babyhood.
Deep in the crimson wine of truth the sixth soft rose
was dyed.
The last was bright with golden light — long may its
joy abide!

And as I looked I knew full well no land more fair
could be.
And angels stooped from paradise that flower-crowned
face to see,
And all who wandered there were blest all blessed
dreams above,
For the land was decked for earth's elect, and the spirit's
name was Love.

WITH FOLDED WINGS.

I LEFT the heaven of heavens this morn,
 Ere yet this morn begun —
A thousand times the earth has borne
 Her burden round the sun
Since to-day broke in heaven and, blest,
We sang the hymn God loveth best.

The silver wings were like a sea
 Sparkling beneath the throne,
Whose mighty billows dazzled me,
 Speeding to earth alone.
Still in the dark that light shines clear,
Still through the silence do I hear.

Yet heaven is not for me, my love,
 While thou on earth dost bide.
Through hours of years I wait above
 Time's onward flowing tide
Till God shall free thy soul, till thou
Shalt feel the glory round thy brow.

Peace! thou shalt look in vain for me
　　Through all the twilight world.
Beyond the moon, for love of thee,
　　I wait with pinions furled.
Art lonely on the peopled earth?
Mine was thy soul before time's birth.

Nay, seems it strange God wills it so,
　　Bidding us still be twain—
For me the joy, for thee the woe
　　Through creeping years of pain?
Ah, love! thy tears bedim my eyes.
When we are one thou shalt arise.

A PASTEL.

May I wander in your woods, ye warblers? May I wander in your woods?

If you will not walk swiftly, nor flaunt your gaudy parasol beneath us, nor lift your spy-glass to count our feathers.

May I wander in your woods, ye beetles? May I wander in your woods?

If you will not tread heavily, nor pluck the brier-rose where we powder our wings, nor start when the humblebee buzzes.

May I wander in your woods, ye breezes? May I wander in your woods?

If you will not wear stiff robes, nor bare the leafy bough, nor veil your face from our kisses.

May I wander in your woods, ye memories? May I wander in your woods?

If you will not gather the fallen leaves, nor shadow your brow with black, nor burden the air with sighs.

IV

DANCING SONG.

CHORIAMBICS.

COME, love, over the fields, green with the spring's
first kiss!
Dance, love! roses will bloom only to gaze at this.
See there — poised in the blue, deep as the truth, and
pure,
White clouds float into one, cleave, though the winds
allure.

Come, dance far and away into the summer's noon ;
Haste on over the night, strewn with the trailing moon.
Ween not love is a sigh, weighted with wings of lead ;
Hear me — love is a dance, light as a seraph's tread.

Ah, sweet! far in the light, storming the gates of pearl,
Two birds circle and wheel, quiver and float and whirl.
Borne on music above soul flies to soaring soul —
What bird singing of love e'er could his wings control ?

So we, what should we know, e'en though the sun
   should die,
Stars dim into the dark — why should you care, or I?
Dance on ! Love is the light, love is immortal bliss.
Life fades into the night — death is love's morning kiss.

MARRIAGE SONG.

BRING roses, bring lilies,
   Wreathe garlands along ;
And in tune with the wedding-bells
   Ho, for a song !

Haste, ye Cupids, come dancing,
   And laugh in your pride,
For the maiden you humbled
   To-day is a bride.

Steal her blushes to redden
   Bright clouds at the dawn.
Bear her sighs where the souls
   Of dead blossoms have gone.

Let her smiles be the gems
   In your coronal prize.
Ah ! but what will ye do
   With the light in her eyes ?

You might set it above
   In the blue ; but a star
Can shine only through darkness,
   And only afar.

A soft sunbeam it were,
   But the sun in his might
Departs with his legions
   At touch of the night.

Oh, what light is so radiant,
   So steadfast and pure,
That when worlds are but ghosts
   It will ever endure?

It is love.   Love alone
   Shines forever and aye.
'T is the light of God's throne,
   'T is the infinite day.

Open wide, then, the gates
   For the bridegroom and bride!
To the land where love waits
   Open wide! open wide!

SLUMBER SONG.

Ah, let me sleep!
The portals of the night close o'er mine eyes;
My spirit in the soothing shadow lies,
    Too tired to weep.

    I see afar
The soft parade of unremembered dreams
Luring me down smooth lotus-wreathéd streams
    Where perfumes are.

    Canst thou not hear
The lulling winds that fan away the day?
The sun sleeps in some cavern far away —
    Why should we fear?

    If he uproll
The curtains of the night and come again,
Then shall we wake in rapture. Hush till then —
    Sleep—sleep, my soul.

LOVE SONG.

MORE lovely is my love
  Than yonder dove
    Who flies so free.
Her voice is sweeter far
  Than larks' notes are.
    Ah, dear is she.

She sitteth in the sun,
  And every one
    Smiles up to God—
As when a lily rare
  Springeth for prayer
    Out of the sod.

Her hair enweaves the light
  In woof as bright
    As saints' brows wear.
Her soul through morning eyes
  Explores the skies,
    For truth is there.

Blest with glad thoughts, she waits
   At life's swung gates
      The call of love —
God's love or man's — ah me !
   How white is she —
      My flower, my dove !

How white is she ! O heart,
   Craven thou art.
      Hark thee — be stilled !
The highest ranks of heaven —
   God's circles seven —
      Christ's love hath filled.

God hath no need of her;
   She does not stir
      When wide skies shine.
She lives for love. Awhile
   Her solemn smile
      Is ours — is mine !

TO A CHILD.

Ah, Margaret, my valentine,
Earth's richest treasures all are thine.
The dawn is in thy glowing hair,
    And in thine eyes
    Are darkening skies,
A-sparkle with the evening star.

Thy voice is like the wakening laugh
Of summer, when the robins quaff
Love-potions with a flight of song.
    Thy footsteps all
    Like daisies fall
Life's shadowy, leafy path along.

And so in loving thee I love
The sweetest thoughts of God above.
An angel's message is thy kiss.
    My valentine,
    Still half divine,
Stoop to me from thy skies of bliss!

LOVE'S POWER.

Who has so fair a face?
Where blooms so rare a grace?
What song so blithe in all the world is ringing?
Meseems my lady spies
My world from azure skies,
Whence sunny wealth of smiles her soul is flinging.

She is so bright, so free,
She cannot stoop to me,
Whom God hath chained to earth, whose soul is craven.
I love her, yet my feet
To flee from her are fleet.
I love her, yet my spirit shuns its haven.

I love her, yet I know
She is more pure than snow,
And I am stained with life, and scarred with warring.
How should I dare to stand
Where seraphs hand in hand
Kneel all agaze, the gates of heaven unbarring?

Yet if she bade me rise
And meet her glowing eyes,
Bade me be brave, earth and the darkness spurning,
My soul would dare to wield
God's sword and bear His shield,
And find that heaven for which the world is yearning.

AU REVOIR.

Forget me not, thou who shalt wander far.
  Here on thy breast I lay
Flowers blue as heaven, enclosing each a star;
  Now onward be thy way!

I do not fear to send thee to the light,
  Though round God's triple throne
Immortal beauty dwells in souls more bright
  Than joy could make mine own.

Though worlds on worlds in marshalled glory shine,
  All singing as they roll,
The seal love set upon thy life is mine.
  I greet thy wakened soul.

Learn on! and when I dare to follow thee
  Beyond death's blinding sun,
Show me God's truth, where souls may wander free,
  When love and light are one.

HOPE.

WHAT wilt thou do when faith is fled
  And hope is dead
  And love's wing broken ?
Wilt thou lie in the grave of the past and sleep,
  While the mourners weep
  And sad rites are spoken ?

Nay, nay — fare forth, though the night be black
  And the storm's red rack
  In the sky is burning ;
For the sun shines somewhere, from gloom released,
  And the heart of the east
  For the day is yearning.

UNFULFILLED.

Lord, I am weak, and through the night
Bright stars stream mercilessly strong.
Where is my will ?   In nebulous flight
Its wide wings drift and waft along,
And dip their trailing plumes in gloom,
And bear me floating far away
Where the deep darkness offers room
For conquering suns to form and sway.

Long trails of shadowy light diffused
That wander dimly through the spheres,
My errant longings, deep infused
With glories of unnumbered years,
Watch at the massing of the suns,
Feel the round planets rolling by,
Lingering while the world-stream runs,
While constellations glow and die.

Ah, Lord ! this nebulous mist of light
That shines not though it searches far —
Canst thou not crush its tangled flight,
Condense its dim glow to a star?
Gather its sweeping subtile wings,
So weary with their wide desire,
And 'mid thy starry lightenings
Count one more shining point of fire.

PROH PUDOR !

A MYSTIC poet sang of valiant knight
And fierce adventure on heroic field,
Where smiling victory ever crowned the wight
Armed well in holiness, whose shining shield
His Lord had tempered.   As my spirits yield
To the sweet, noble harmony, I know
The joy of great achievement, seem to wield
The hero's conquering lance, and strike the blow
At error's heart which shall uncoil her folds of woe.

Ah, sad awakening ! Spenser, if thou were
This cycle's epic bard, thy joyous lay
Would be attuned to mourning.   In the stir
And smoke of life, the singers of to-day
Seek not to crown the victor, nor to lay
The muses' wreath upon a hero's grave,
But rearward of the race their stars, astray,
Illume with ugly truth some straggling slave,
And leave to darkness and forgetfulness the brave.

Have we no majesty, no beauty still
To make the new tales worthy of the old?
Strong have our deeds been ; let our strength but fill
Volumes with pæans, that our age, so bold,
May, like the sun, set in a blaze of gold,
Kindling the world to glory !   Then at last
The child of a great morrow shall behold
Advance the flaming banners of the past
Across the somber dawn of times undreamed and vast.

FOR JOHN PAUL

Who sent roses on St. Valentine's day.

STAY, sweet roses, stay but a day,
Breathe me your souls ere your leaves decay,
That over the air to my valentine
I may waft him a perfume as rich as wine,
That shall charm his desire to some dear repose
As safe and as sweet as thy heart, white rose !

TO ROBERT LOUIS STEVENSON.

In wet wood and miry lane
Still we pound and pant in vain.

*From the lines " To Will H. Low "
in " Underwoods."*

VAIN the outstretched hands, the feet
Blistered in the noonday heat ;
Vain the climbing thought, the brain
Dull with longing —all are vain.

Eyes of seer may never see
Semblance of his ecstasy.
Poet's arms shall ne'er embrace
Beauty, whose averted face
Lures him to a hopeless chase.

Yet who seeks her shall behold
Trails of glory, fields of gold,
Till the splendor of her eyes
Leads his soul to paradise.

Ah, pursue her still ! for we,
Gazing where thou searchest, see
Crystal flashes of her wings,
Glimpses of celestial things.

OUTWARD BOUND.

Let time and the waves roll by
   To their haven over the sea —
My bark is my home, say I,
   My love is my life to me.

My love is my life — ah, woe !
   Sail on, for the skies are blue.
Sail on, while the glad winds blow —
   My love as my life is true.

Worlds lie in yon golden star
   More young than the burning sun.
I follow my love afar !
   Nay — death and life are one.

TO HESTER.

Thou art so still !
My heart's blood freezes 'neath thy frosty will.
Thine eyes, as constant as the polar star,
Are colder far.

Ah, not for thee
The ardor of the south, where love is free.
The sun allows thee but a polar ray —
An arctic day.

A star must woo
Far through the soundless heaven's serenest blue —
Bright Arcturus or dauntless Antares —
Thy soul to please.

And such as I,
Whose love is all my immortality,
Dream what were his, what bliss of gods above,
Whom thou shouldst love !

EPITAPH ON A DOG.

He has fled from life, and we
Soon his followers shall be.
Even a dog's death may recall
Death's sure conquest of us all.

Even a dog! — ah, well may we
Death's dark hour with calmness see,
If our lives as his have been
Loving, faithful, brave, serene.

A QUESTION.

Do I love her, say you? Why
   Will you give a stately name
To a mood that wanders by
Like a perfume? Love her? Ay!
   Do you blame?

You have rigid rules. You know
   All the haunts of duty. There,
Where the armored lilies glow
None shall see you bending low —
   Ah, beware!

Yours the loss! Look — she doth shine
   Like a chalice crowned with flowers,
Brimming with ambrosial wine
Brewed in joy for lips divine —
   Not for ours.

Yet my soul is mirrored there
   Golden as the blessed sun.
Shall I quaff the goblet? Where
Were my dream then? I forbear.
   Who has won?

A SKETCH.

ALERT and over-wise,
The spirit in her eyes
Laughs at our weary sighs,
    Our fierce endeavor.
For, scan it as she may,
This life is but a play
That fools us for a day,
    Then stops forever.

Philosophies she reads,
And dabbles with the creeds,
And gloats upon the deeds
    Of saint and sinner.
So young! she dares to know
All that the world may show,
And never feel a throe
    The heart within her.

Yet rare she is, and sweet.
Methinks some seraph fleet
Her brave adventurous feet
    Is softly guiding;

Who o'er her eyelids flings
Shadows of folded wings,
The abyss of evil things
    Tenderly hiding.

Perchance, for pity's sake,
Some golden morn will break
And bid the soul awake
    Now idly sleeping.
Some light of love or truth,
Some fire of pain or ruth
Will flash upon her youth,
    In lowlands creeping.

For her, then, through the blue
Worlds will be born anew,
And light divine shine true
    Thick clouds now darken.
And out of dull disguise
A spirit will arise
Fit to explore the skies,
    At heaven's gate harken.

.

A DAUGHTER OF THE DAKOTAS.

SLEEP softly, O my mother !
The wind has died away
That stirred the silent waves of mist,
Where beckoning shadows play.

Wrapped in her fleecy blanket,
The moon has gone to rest ;
The wigwams stand like warrior ghosts
To guide me on my quest.

My vows ye would not listen,
My tears ye would not heed ;
Sleep on, and let the stars alone
Behold my valiant deed.

.   .   .   .   .

The night enfolds me softly,
My steps are light as dew ;
I do not fear the spirits near,
My steel is strong and true.

277

They sold me to the sorcerer
And bade my love despair —
My brave who wears the eagle's plumes
Above his shining hair.

I clad me in my splendor,
My fringéd robes and beads,
And met him by the river brink
Among the swaying reeds.

I told him of my dreaming:
When sleep had made me strong
The Spirit of the Waters* rose
And sang a battle-song;

And bade my soul have courage,
And gave me power divine
To strike the cruel wizard-chief,
His enemy and mine —

His foe who dared to wander
With Thunder through the air,
Who scourged the Waters and unloosed
Fierce lightnings from his lair.

---

* In the mythology of the Dakotas the Spirit of the Winds and
the Spirit of the Waters were perpetually at war, and they engaged
mortals in their service.

My troth once more I plighted,
   My vows once more I swore.
For I will wed my love ; the chief
   We fear shall live no more.

My brave across the prairies
   I sent with spear and bow
Lest they should slay him for the blood
   My knife alone shall know.

Deep be its stroke !   To-morrow
   They will not braid my hair,
Nor deck my brow with silver gauds
   Fit for a bride to wear.

And through the days of mourning
   Glad will I be and free,
Till in the moon of ripening rice
   My love shall come to me.

         .   .   .   .   .

Bravely the night has sped me,
   The curtain waves me in.
How black he lies, this bridegroom wise,
   All withered with his sin !

Great Spirit of the Waters —
  Now clothe mine arm with power!
Against thy foe I strike this blow,
  Whose soul is thine this hour.

Even though the flying tempest
  Should beat his thunder wings,
I will not fear, for thou art near —
  I hear thy murmurings.

BY THE DRAGON RIVER.

Fair wreaths upon cold altars lie.
  Ah, lovely vows are said and sung
That echoless but rise and die,
  And give the wandering winds no tongue.

Brave vows ! But yesterday, they say,
  A troop of maidens slender-eyed,
Pale as their yellow sun's last ray,
  Vowed to live pure, and stainless died.

Vowed to live pure beneath the moon
  In that sere land where love is naught,
Where maids with flowery hearts of June
  Like autumn fruits are sold and bought.

And when one maiden felt her vow
  Falter beneath her sire's command,
Even with the bride-veil on her brow
  Swift fled she to the virgin band.

And loyally they twined their souls
  Into a wreath of lilies white,
To crown the Dragon where it rolls
  Its swift flood through the purple night.

They sang above the torrent dark
  A low sweet song of joy.   Ah me !
The restive winds lay still to hark,
  The almond flowers bowed low to see.

Then from a world to truth unkind,
  Seeking a world where truth is blest,
Together, arms and hearts entwined,
  Downward they leaped.   God knows the rest.

A HYMN.

THY bounty is a crystal well
    Where all the world may drink.
We bring bright cups, and can not tell
    What waits us at the brink.

One quaffs rich draughts of joy ; and one,
    Lifting his strong arm high,
Some dear pledge shouting to the sun,
    Drains sorrow's chalice dry.

And one, wreathing his bowl for sleep,
    Quaffs years of bitter breath ;
And one, hope's beaker dipping deep,
    ' Tastes the wide seas of death.

Yet crystal clear the waters rise
    From infinite realms of rest ;
Each cup mirrors the glowing skies,
    And every drop is blest.

SONNETS

TO MY LEADER.

THE years have surged o'er life's receding shore —
Soft waves from Time's vast ocean — since with thee
I walked in joy, since thou revealed to me
Glories my soul had never known before.
Once I was blind : o'er dull eyes thou didst pour
The glowing gift of light, eternal, free.
Lo ! I was dumb : thou spak'st of liberty
And straight my mind shattered the chains it wore.
All that is best in me is thine.   Thou art
My inspiration, as of old the star
Conjured its worshiper to song.   The goal
Of thy sure hope so lofty is, thy heart
So pure, I can but love thee from afar —
My friend, my sister, mother of my soul.

TO A CLASS-MATE.

DOST thou remember days when thou and I
Walked thoughtful o'er the violet-studded green —
When oaks waved high above us, and between
We searched the deep blue beauty of the sky?
Life smiled about us then; with visions high
Gay we invoked the future. Each was queen
Of a wide realm of fancies, and the sheen
Of youth's gold splendor o'er the world did lie.
Alas! we meet no more. The gathering years
Are eloquent with silence, and thy face
Is but a memory. But the thought of thee,
Of our vague dreams, our faith that banished fears,
Is like a benediction, and the grace
Of the old blesséd time comes back to me.

TIME'S PERVERSITY.

O Time, how cunning are thy ways with men!
Along the blooming road thou liest prone
In ambush, and when youth dreams all his own
Thy hoar hand smites, and all the summer then
Turns ashen, and life's flushing glories wane,
Shrivel to age before thy gaze of stone.
Thou art unmerciful, for many a moan
Thou smotherest with the dust of years of pain,
But dost not comfort.   Me thou mockest, Time.
Thou wav'st me past the garden-land of song,
Where I would weave thee garlands all the day,
And bid'st me pave with stones thy stubborn way,
Till my sad soul doth oft for blindness long,
For freedom from a vision too sublime.

ON READING A MODERN ROMANCE.

Across the shadow of these morbid years,
Whose growth luxuriant, tangled, loads the air
With perfume and decay; whose soil doth bear
Rich rottenness, while rooted beauty rears
Heaven-seeking boughs through a hot mist of tears —
Oh, through this breathless region let the blast
From happier centuries sweep pure and fast
And strong upon our fever and our fears!
Hark! the clear voice of man's imperial youth
Cries warning to his weary middle age —
Sings of the days when newly found was truth,
Nor blasted yet by doubting Time's bleak rage;
When men bowed low to nature, holiest shrine
Of God, and, rising, knew they were divine.

" THE MONARCH."

A portrait of a lion, by Rosa Bonheur, now in the Vanderbilt collection.

NAY, wouldst thou rule — thou impotent, fond man?
Lo — I am here.   What wilt thou do with me,
Thou and thy past? — thy vagrant memory ;
Thy wisdom that would impudently scan
The universe ; thy hope, that longs to span
The unborn centuries, that dares decree
Laws for the Infinite !   Ah, hush thy plea,
For I am here.   Obliterate thy plan.
The tassel dangling from the throne of Truth
Is all that thou canst reach — why wilt thou climb?
Why wilt thou spend thy soul, and waste thy youth
In passionate consciousness ?   Ah ! fool sublime !
Wisdom and power are mine, the eternal Now
Am I.   Thou puny thinker, what art thou ?

AN INVOCATION TO HEALTH.

For one seeking her in the Adirondacks.

COME, spirit of life ! Far in the blue serene,
Where spent desire sleepeth in deeps of light,
Why dost thou linger still ? The noiseless night,
The dying year, the desolate soft sheen
Of moonlit snows wrapping the world and e'en
The winds in robes of silence, and the might
Of sleeping pulses prisoned — all invite
The swift thrill of thy breath, for thou art queen.
Come to thy votary, that not in vain
He climb the trackless reaches of the snow
In search of thee. Pour thine ethereal wine
Through all his weariness, till mocking pain
Flee like a phantom, that his soul may know
Freedom to wander far in fields divine !

TO MRS. YALE.

FRIEND, let me wait still longer at thy feet
Thanking thee silently for perfect things:
For antique doors flung open, for the wings
Of orioles in the fruit-trees, for the seat
By the broad hearth, sacred with memories sweet;
For portraits of dead youth, whose beauty clings
Still to loved walls; for high imaginings
Won from old songs where gods and mortals meet.
But most for thee let me thank God and thee,
Whom time delights to honor, whose long youth
Feels not the snowy fall of wintry years.
Blest as yon mighty elm, of gifts as free,
Thy soul strives ever nearer to the truth,
Ever more tenderly earth's voices hears.

Deerfield, July the third, 1891.

TO MY SISTER.

From over the Sea.

I FEEL thy hand upon my heart, I see
Thy white brow bending softly over mine.
Thy voice is in mine ear, thy deep eyes shine
Like stars above me.   Thou hast followed me,
For spirit and desire alike are free.
The invulnerable ocean doth entwine
Its strong white arms about my love and thine,
Guarding them safely for eternity.
Seas can not part us, nor the soundless deep
Where Time casts down the treasures of the earth —
The perishable baubles we adore.
Our souls shall wake from this abyss of sleep,
To feel the rapture of a strange new birth,
Walk hand in hand with Truth forevermore.

RED CLOVER.

Call me new-born thy worshiper, sweet flower,
Soft laughter of the meadows! I have seen
Thy pink spheres shake away the dewy screen
From night's caress to greet the dawn's glad hour.
I feel the rich weight of thy blossoms cower,
When wild winds sweep across the wastes of green,
Startling the bees, who, restful wings a-sheen,
Steal thy sweet riches for their queen's bright dower.
Thou seem'st to all pure things allied, and so
Thy blossoms touched no stranger when they lay
So proudly 'neath that rose-tipped chin of hers.
For she, though bred in cities, yet doth know
The finer thoughts of nature. Her soul stirs
To greet thee as thine own to greet the day.

TO A BEAUTIFUL LADY.

WHENAS my soul lies brimming like a well
And sweetest thoughts rise bubbling to the brink ;
When floating flowers upon my fancy dwell
And the blue sky deep in mine heart doth sink
Full-mirrored ; when swift joys alight and drink
Supernal draughts, till, burdened like a bell,
They cleave the hush with song, and dare not shrink
From sunward flights to glory's citadel :
Then do I think on thee, and hark to hear
A choir of seraphs striking harps divine ;
For thou art pure as waters crystal-clear,
Lovely as lilies, as soft rains benign.
Of God's high purposes and life's deep cheer
Thy soul the proof is, and thy face the sign.

TO W. S. M.

With a copy of Shelley.

BEHOLD, I send thee to the heights of song,
My brother ! Let thine eyes awake as clear
As morning dew, within whose glowing sphere
Is mirrored half a world ; and listen long,
Till in thine ears, famished to keenness, throng
The bugles of the soul — till far and near
Silence grows populous, and wind and mere
Are phantom-choked with voices. Then be strong —
Then halt not till thou seest the beacons flare
Souls mad for truth have lit from peak to peak.
Haste on to breathe the intoxicating air —
Wine to the brave and poison to the weak —
Far in the blue where angels' feet have trod,
Where earth is one with heaven, and man with God.

.

BY LAKE MICHIGAN.

Blue as eternity, bright as God's smile,
Pure as the folded wings of seraphim,
Thy waters flow this morning at the rim
Of paradise. Full many a mile on mile
Some golden craft might bear me to the isle
Where solemn Sappho sings her sacred hymn,
Where love is ever young, eyes never dim,
And truth a shining splendor all the while.
Surely my soul might sail into thy blue,
And be so purged of earthly dross and stain
That one I loved would take the form I knew,
And speak to me and clasp my hand again,
Stooping with wingéd throngs for retinue
From the wide heaven where he hath learned
    to reign.

ENVOI

ENVOI.

On reading Longfellow's lines "The Arrow and the Song."

ALTHOUGH my arrow miss its goal,
    And all my song be lost in air,
Yet I have aimed the shaft; my soul
    Has known of song the sweet despair.

What though amid the choral throng
    Who feel the lightning of thy breath,
Bright Muse, and, sowing earth with song,
    Pass on to fame through gates of death —

I cannot stand, sun-crowned, on high!
    Yet at the mountain's shadowy base
At times may glories daze mine eye,
    Far-away glimpses of thy face.

Ah! then, when all my thought is free
    From care, that now the vision blurs,
Gladness my soul shall know, to be
    Even least among thy worshipers.

www.ingramcontent.com/pod-product-compliance
Lightning Source LLC
Chambersburg PA
CBHW031403270326
41929CB00010BA/1300